WordPress To Go

How To Build A WordPress Website On Your Own Domain, From Scratch, Even If You Are A Complete Beginner

Sarah McHarry

WordPress To Go

ISBN-13: 978-1481130509

For Edward

Table of Contents

Introduction

Welcome!

Welcome to this WordPress beginner's guide.

You are about to join thousands of other webmasters who have used this book to build their own WordPress websites, from scratch, even if they were complete beginners!

Before we start, let's make one thing quite clear. This book is deliberately short. That's because I want to take you through the basics of building your own website in the quickest manner possible.

I want you to learn speedily without getting distracted by non-essentials or trivia. Sure, you can buy a 1,000-page bumper WordPress guide that will turn you into a world-authority(!) but it won't help you get online any quicker.

One of the secrets of what used to be known as the 'new technology' is that, if you concentrate on the basic essentials, it isn't nearly as difficult as it seems. The truth is that much of the tricky-sounding technical detail can be ignored when you are first starting. First, get through a few crucial first steps and then it gradually gets easier.

You'll find that there is a bit of a learning curve when you first start, but that soon evens out as you get going. As with any unfamiliar discipline, the more you learn the simpler it becomes.

What I will promise you is that, if you follow along the lessons in this book, do exactly as I tell you (!), step by step, then you'll end up with your very own website that you built yourself, even if this is the first time you have ever ventured into the online world.

Why should I build my own website when I can easily get online for free?

Having your own web presence is now pretty much essential in today's online world. Even teenage kids have their own pages on sites such as Facebook and the many other social networks. Services like Blogspot, Weebly, Squidoo - and many more - offer free web space to anyone who wants it. Anyone with an Internet connection can now easily get themselves on to the web for free.

But the problem is that these free site-building services can come and go, change the rules as they go and impose restrictions. Some free services can shut your site down if they don't approve of your content.

Many will clutter up your site with trashy ads and your free site can disappear overnight if the service goes bust or gets taken over. And they offer little or no technical support when you really need it.

So why should I build my own website on my own domain?

The answer is that, with your own privately registered domain and hosting account, YOU own and control the website, not anybody else. You can put whatever you like on your site (within the bounds of legality) and no-one can tell you otherwise. You are your own boss.

And, with your own website, you can build your own distinctive 'brand', whether you are a business or a community group, an individual, or whatever... You can make your site look and behave how you like, whether for e-commerce, or for publicity purposes, as an information resource - or just a personal blog.

Your domain becomes your very own exclusive web address, your own piece of online virtual 'real estate' that plays its part in publicizing your mission or message.

These days, if you don't have your own online web presence, you are invisible.

You can print your domain address on your business cards, add it to your email signature and quote in all your offline literature. Your own website on your own domain gives you identity, visibility and, indeed, status.

But don't I need a professional web designer to make a good job of building a website?

No, definitely not! This used to be the case in the early days of the Internet because only a few tech-savvy geeks knew and understood the computer language (HTML) that translated your words and pictures into the code that browsers understand.

But as the technology has advanced, so have the tools to build websites become more accessible. WordPress is one of these tools and WordPress is the subject of this book.

What if I'm not a technical wizard – will I understand all the jargon about web-building?

With this book you don't need to know any jargon or gobbledygook – I explain it all in plain English as we go along. As you use the system it will begin to click into place and you'll understand what you need to know and what you don't.

If you can use a word processor you can build your own WordPress website – it's that simple - I promise!

How much will it cost to do it all myself?

Peanuts. The only thing you absolutely have to spend money on is web hosting and you can get this for a few dollars a month.

For less than $10 per month you can get your web hosting account from one of the top hosting companies on the planet.

Sure, you can spend money on other tools and services if you want, but, for a simple website that you build yourself you really don't need to spend any more money than that.

What Is WordPress?

WordPress is a powerful (and free!) package of software that sits in the background on your web server (the remote computer where your domain is hosted) and performs all the technical processing that delivers your content to your visitor on their local computer. Once WordPress is installed on your domain you don't need to do anything to make it work. It just sits there and performs its magic entirely behind the scenes.

WordPress provides a WYSIWYG ('what you see is what you get') interface to the webmaster (you!) that bypasses the need to know any HTML, PHP, CSS, JavaScript, MySQL or any other coding language.

Once the hangout of hobbyists and bloggers, WordPress has now evolved into a powerful and sophisticated web platform that supports a host of features both for professional and do-it-yourself webmasters.

The terms 'blog' and 'website' are now effectively synonymous as far as our usage of WordPress is concerned. Pundits use the two terms inter-changeably because the technology platform behind both is exactly the same.

WordPress is now actually used by some of the major players on the Internet as a complete Content Management System (CMS). Think CNN, The New York Times, About.com, the White House, US Post Office, and Ford Motors - they all make use of WordPress.

And, in addition to the experts, millions of ordinary people and small businesses around the world also use WordPress as their platform of choice to get a presence on the web.

What's so special about WordPress?

- WordPress is FREE and open-source

- WordPress is stable and maintained by experts

- WordPress contains numerous behind-the-scenes features that make creating your own website a breeze

WordPress is wonderful, but it has a reputation for being difficult. This is, in part, due to the documentation.

WordPress was originally written by programmers, for programmers, and the instructions ('codex', as it's termed) are often written in tech-speak and seem to assume that you know what they are talking about in the first place. This has improved in recent versions, but it can still be a challenge if you are not a fully paid-up techie.

I know all this. I'm a computer programmer myself. I actually am a techie (and proud of it!) but I can also write plain English. In this tutorial, I just concentrate on the basic essentials of WordPress and ignore all the complications that you don't need to know when you're first starting out.

How To Use This Tutorial

The best way to use this tutorial is to sit down at your PC with this book beside you and follow each lesson, step by step.

Because WordPress is now so sophisticated and flexible, it can sometimes be difficult for newcomers to see the wood from the trees. So I have broken this tutorial down into two levels:

- Quick Start Guide

- In-Depth Guide

The Quick Start Guide, covering Lessons 1 – 8, is intended to get you up and running, building your own WordPress website, mostly using the default settings, and avoiding as many of the technicalities as possible.

When you have completed lessons 1 – 8 you will have a basic, working website that you can continue to build and use without any further tweaking. For many people, this is all they may ever need.

The In-Depth Guide takes you further than just the basics and introduces some of the more sophisticated and functional options that WordPress provides to help you make your website more efficient and unique. Lessons 9 – 20 take the basic website that you built in the Quick Start Guide and help you develop it on to become a feature-rich resource, tailored for your purposes.

You may not need to do all the lessons in In-Depth Guide: you can just dip in and out to find what you need to know, as you choose.

FAQs (Frequently Asked Questions) appear at the end of each lesson and cover the main queries people often ask when they've read the lesson. The FAQs may not be relevant to you but they could just add a little bit of extra know-how when it is needed.

When you've completed all twenty lessons you will have learned all the basics of building a WordPress website. You'll be well-equipped to discover for yourself any of the more advanced features that you may wish to investigate.

Right, let's get started!

QUICK START GUIDE – YOUR OWN WEBSITE IN 8 EASY LESSONS

Lesson 1. Register Your Domain And Sign Up For Web Hosting

This is the first step to getting your own web presence. But if you already have a domain and hosting account you can skip this lesson and go on to Lesson 2.

As I've already stated, this is the first and only place in this tutorial where you will need to spend any money. Having a reliable company to host your website is an essential investment and it doesn't cost mega-bucks. Once you have your hosting account set up you can forget all about the very complex communications technology needed to support your website because you're paying somebody to provide it for you. And, I promise you, if you go with the web hosting company that I recommend, you will get a very good deal indeed.

If you have never done any of this before and you're a bit intimidated by all the jargon and tech-speak, don't panic. There is a mass of incomprehensible gobbledygook associated with web hosting and Internet technology but the good news is that you don't need to understand nor care about most of it. Let me take you by the hand and I will explain just what you do need to know as we go along. To coin a cliché, it's not rocket science. Trust me.

When you've completed this lesson you will have taken your first giant leap into the online world of web-building…

Choose Your Domain

OK, to begin, you need to decide on a domain. Your domain name is your unique web address and it's what people will type into their browser to reach your website. So it's a good idea to make it a name that's easy to remember and easy to spell and that tells people what your website is all about. So what sort of domain name should you have?

Ideally, you want the domain name to indicate to people what your site is all about. It is better to have a domain like 'keepingchickens.com' rather than 'xyz101.com' because it spells out to your customers, and the search engines, precisely what your site is about. But your domain could be your own name or nickname, or your business name or maybe a slogan that describes your mission.

The .com extension is the most universally recognized suffix to a domain name, but you could also have .net or .org, the latter especially if you are a non-business organization. The .net extension can be handy if the .com version of your domain is already taken. And there's also .us, .co, .biz, .info (and more) if you want to look different. Plus, there are the country-specific domain name extensions such as .uk, .au, .de - it's your call.

Sign Up For Web Hosting

The hosting company that I recommend for WordPress websites is Hostgator (www.hostgator2go.com). They have an awesome reputation for reliability and customer service and they also offer very competitive pricing. And they have the added advantage that they provide a handy script for automatically installing WordPress on your domain. This is really useful – installing WordPress manually can be a minefield even if you do know what you're doing (you can tell I learned that the hard way, can't you?)

Hostgator offers several hosting plans and you can sign up for periods of between 1 month and 3 years. If you sign up for 1 month you will pay your hosting fees monthly. If you sign up for 1 year you will pay your hosting fees annually. As you might expect, the longer you sign up for, the cheaper it becomes. And you can pay via credit/debit card or PayPal.

Figure 1.1

So, to set up your WordPress hosting with Hostgator, go to www.hostgator2go.com (Figure 1.1), click anywhere on the front page and then choose 'shared hosting' when the 'Select You Type of Hosting' drop-down box appears. Then Click 'Continue'.

Now you have to choose which hosting plan you want.

- The' Hatchling' is the very cheapest plan, allowing you to host just one domain on the service.

- The 'Baby' plan is essentially the same service as the Hatchling but with the Baby you can host an unlimited number of domains on the same account without paying any extra.

This is for you to decide. If you decide to start off with Hatchling, you can upgrade to Baby if you want to at some time in the future.

Hostgator has a habit of offering amazing discounts on their services and these may vary from time to time. But if you quote the coupon code 'HOSTBOOK25' Hostgator will know that you are a reader of this book and they will give you the maximum possible discount available at the time!

So, choose either the 'Hatchling' or 'Baby' plan and click on 'Order Now'. Enter your chosen domain name and don't forget to enter HOSTBOOK25 as the coupon code.

Then follow the prompts to complete the purchase process. I recommend that you select privacy protection for your domain because this hides your identity from spammers.

You did it! You've nearly completed Lesson 1.

You've got your domain and a hosting account. When you've signed up with Hostgator, check your email. You'll receive an email from them with your account sign-in and password. It's a good idea to keep this email (or even print it out) so that you have a record of your hosting details.

For security reasons Hostgator may want to telephone you after you register to verify that you are the person who opened the account, so please provide them with an easily accessible phone number. (Or they might ask you to call them).

Don't worry; they won't try to sell you anything: all they want is to know that the account was opened by you (or with your permission) and that you are a real person and not a robot. This step is essential before you can access your account and get started.

In the remainder of this tutorial I'm going to take you through the creation of a WordPress website using my domain '1.keepingchickens. net' as an example. I'll start right at the beginning and you'll watch the website unfold, lesson by lesson. If you work alongside me, you can build your own site at the same pace.

Lesson 2 assumes that you are starting out with a Hostgator hosting account and that you don't have the WordPress software installed already.

I'll show you how to install WordPress with just a few clicks of the mouse and then you'll be all set to begin building a WordPress website!

FAQ

I live in the UK and I would rather use a UK-based hosting company. Do I have to use the American Hostgator?

No, I can recommend a company called JustHost who are based in the UK. They offer .uk domain names (as well as those above) and all billing is in GBP (pounds sterling).

Figure 1.2

JustHost provides high-quality, low-priced hosting equivalent to the Hostgator Hatchling plan and their user-interface is very similar so you should be able to follow this tutorial without any trouble.

To use JustHost go to www.justhost4u.com (Figure 1.2) and click the 'Sign-Up' button.

I already have a domain that I registered with another registrar. Can I still use the domain with Hostgator?

Yes – you can still set up Hostgator hosting for a pre-registered domain but, in these circumstances, you must change your domain's Domain Name Servers (DNS) to indicate that your website will be hosted on Hostgator.

This is necessary so that the domain name system (which drives the Internet) can translate your domain name into a specific IP (Internet Protocol) address that identifies the specific bit of hardware that hosts your website. I admit that that sounds a bit technical but it's really quite simple.

All you've got to do is change two fields on your domain registrar's screen and you're done. Here's how.

When you sign up for a Hostgator hosting account you will receive a welcome email which will tell you what name servers to use. This will be a pair of codes that look like ns????.hostgator.com (where???? are numbers allocated by Hostgator).

You will need to log into your account at the registrar you used when you bought the domain. There should be somewhere fairly obvious on their screen labeled 'Set your DNS' (or something like that). Enter the two codes Hostgator supplied and save the settings.

The changes may take place immediately or you may have to wait several hours (or more) before you can access the domain at Hostgator. This is because the information has to propagate out to all the networks on the Internet that need to know where to find your website and this is not always immediate.

If you can't find out how to change your DNS then try accessing your registrar's FAQ page or knowledgebase. If all else fails, contact their Tech Support and ask them to help.

Lesson 2. Install WordPress On Your Domain

What we're going to do now is install the WordPress software on your domain and hosting account. The good news is that you only have to do this once, so just get through this step and you're on your way to a great website!

I have given instructions here for Hostgator. If you have a hosting account with another provider, check whether they have the cPanel (stands for 'control panel') interface. If so, this set of instructions will likely apply to your host, too.

If you are with a different host and they don't have cPanel, ask their Technical Support for instructions on how to install WordPress.

Install WordPress With 'Quickinstall'

If you're still with me, log in to Hostgator with the username and password that they emailed to you. You will be passed on to the cPanel interface (Figure 2.1). This is where you access all the resources and services that Hostgator provides for you.

Figure 2.1

Scroll down this page until you see the section headed 'Software/Services' (Figure 2.2).

Figure 2.2

Click on 'QuickInstall' and then on the 'WordPress' link under 'Blog Software'.

Figure 2.3

Then click 'Continue' and you'll see a screen like the one in Figure 2.3. Enter the name of your domain alongside 'http://' and then enter your email, the title of your website and your first and last name. This is the minimum information WordPress needs to create a website. You can change any of this information later. Then click 'Install Now!' and wait for the script to finish.

Then it's done. WordPress is installed on your domain - easy peasy! Check your email to get your WordPress username and password.

If all this went well, congratulations - you can now skip to the next lesson.

Install WordPress With 'Fantastico'

If you don't have access to QuickInstall you can use the other tool called 'Fantasico' to install WordPress automatically. There are several versions of this tool so what you see may vary slightly from what I am showing you here, but most of it is self-explanatory.

First, click on the icon labeled 'Fantastico'. You'll see this screen in Figure 2.4:

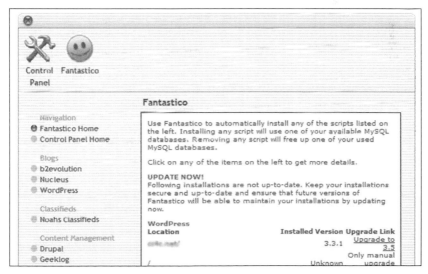

Figure 2.4

Click on 'WordPress' in the left panel. Then on the next screen click 'New Installation'.

Click on your domain name in the drop-down box and then enter your administrator-username and password (can be anything but remember what you typed!), nickname, email address, site name and description. You can change any of these entries later when you log in to your WordPress website. Then click on the 'Install WordPress' button. Wait for a short while and it's done!

Check your email for a confirmation that WordPress has been installed on your domain and save this (or print it out) for security purposes.

———

Congratulations! When you've completed this lesson you have an empty WordPress website on your domain just waiting for you to make it your own!

FAQ

Help! I installed WordPress but I've made a complete mess of everything and I want to start again. Can I uninstall WordPress on my domain?

Yes, you can. Log in to Hostgator's cPanel and go back into QuickInstall (see Figure 2.3).

Click on the button at the top of the screen that says 'Manage Installations'. You will see a small red cross to the right of your domain name. Click this and an option will appear labeled 'Uninstall'.

Follow the prompts and your WordPress installation will disappear. You can then start over.

Lesson 3. How To Log In And Out Of WordPress

Now let's deal with a few of the basics and begin with logging into and out of WordPress.

Log Into WordPress

Whenever you want to work on your website you need to login into WordPress by typing the following into your browser:

http://yourdomain.com/wp-admin (where 'yourdomain.com' is your actual domain name. In my case this is keepingchickens.net)

You'll see the familiar WordPress login screen as in Figure 3.1:

Figure 3.1

Enter the username and password that you were given when you installed WordPress and click 'Log In'.

It's a good idea to bookmark this login because you'll be using it a lot.

If you have a computer-generated password you can change this to something else after we get started. As soon as you feel familiar enough with the WordPress dashboard, go to Lesson 17 and that will explain how to change the log-in password.

When you first log in, you'll be passed to the Dashboard (Figure 3.2) which is where all the action starts:

Figure 3.2

The top of the screen is all about 'Jetpack' which is one of WordPress' latest gizmos which we are not going to use in this tutorial and which we'll deactivate later. So ignore that for the time being.

The welcome messages shown on this screen vary from time so don't worry if the body of your screen looks a little bit different from this.

If you see 'Welcome to WordPress' box, you can click 'Dismiss' in the top right corner of the box because we're not going to use that, either.

What we are really interested in at this stage is the vertical menu down the left-hand side of the screen headed 'Dashboard', which is where all the behind-the-scenes action takes place.

We're going to be using this set of dashboard drop-down menus to access the inner workings of WordPress to build a website. Whenever I say 'from the dashboard…' I will be directing you to click on one of these left-side menu items. I will explain each one that you need to use as we go along.

Updating WordPress

Just a quick digression here. The WordPress development team has an on-going mission to improve and expand its capabilities and they release new versions of the software at regular intervals.

So when you log into your site and see a message above the dashboard saying that a new release of WordPress is available, it's OK to click to update the software.

Just follow the prompts and the update will overwrite the version you currently use. You usually don't need to do anything else but you should check out whether there are new features that you might take advantage of. There will typically be something announced in the body of the dashboard and you can also check out www.wordpress.org for news on the latest release.

And, if you are with Hostgator, they now run an automatic WordPress update whenever a new version is released. They don't always do this immediately but if you don't update your WordPress installation, Hostgator will do it behind the scenes by default.

View Your Website As The World Sees It

Anytime you want to see what your site currently looks like, from the dashboard, hover your mouse over the site title up in the top left corner of the screen and click 'Visit Site'. The whole site will be displayed and you can view it as a visitor will see it. You will have to click the back button to get back to the dashboard.

Log Out Of WordPress

To log out of WordPress, look at the top right corner of the screen where it says 'Howdy ...', hover your mouse over this and click 'Log Out' on the drop-down menu. WordPress logs you out of your website but leaves the log-on box on the screen in case you want to go back in.

FAQ

What about all the other incomprehensible stuff I can see in the body of the dashboard screen?

You can ignore most of it for now, but when you get your website up and going you will find one or two of the panels quite useful. The 'Right Now' panel gives you an up-to-date summary of the status of your website and we'll come to the QuickPress Panel in Lesson 7.

If you really don't want to see the geeky 'WordPress Blog' or 'Other WordPress News' (or any other dashboard panel) then click on 'Screen Options' on the top right of the screen and uncheck these items. They will then disappear.

And, if you want, you can rearrange the panels on the dashboard by clicking and dragging them up and down.

Lesson 4. The Design Of Your WordPress Website

Right then – here's where it starts to get interesting...

The visual appearance of a WordPress website is governed by a design template called a 'theme'. The theme determines the overall appearance and layout of the site, the color scheme, the fonts, and the style – in fact, the whole overall look and feel of the site. Think of it as a 'skin'.

One of the wonders of WordPress is that you can change the theme of your site with a few clicks of the mouse and everything will (usually) click into place with a brand-new visual style.

The default theme provided by WordPress on new installations is the minimalist 'Twenty Twelve' theme, which is what is illustrated below.

Figure 4.1 shows what my Chicken Keeping website looks like straight out of the box:

Figure 4.1

This is the default look and style of Twenty Twelve and I admit that it doesn't look very interesting as yet – but I'm about to change all that.

I'm going to recommend that you stick with this theme to start with as it will be easier to follow the lessons if you do. If you want to, you can change it later when you know what you are doing.

In this lesson I'll show you how to tweak Twenty Twelve so that you can explore for yourself the options that this theme provides.

Sketch Out A Blueprint For Your Website

Before going much further, it would be a good idea for you to sketch out on paper roughly what you want your website to look like and how you want it to behave so that, as we work through the tutorial, you can be putting your design into practice.

Figure 4.2 shows the outline of a typical website and one that Twenty Twelve follows:

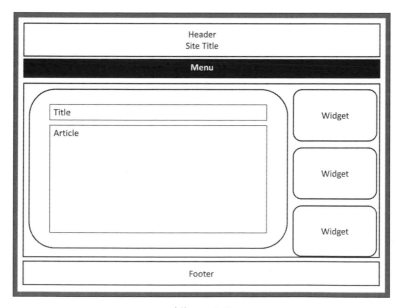

Figure 4.2

What you need to sketch out is what you want to go where and approx imately what you want your site to look like.

At this stage, I suggest you design the layout of your website to be as simple as possible because, if you can live with the simple Twenty Twelve WordPress layout for now, you will find it quicker to build your own site.

The Twenty Twelve architecture provides many of the typical features that are found on most websites:

- The header is at the top of the page and this can be an image, or a block of text, or both. The text would consist of the site title with an optional extra tagline. The header normally appears at the top of every page.

- Below the title is the 'menu' which is a horizontal bar containing tabs which link to the various pages in your website. Twenty Twelve actually puts the menu above the header but many themes put it below.

- The main body of each page contains an article (page or post) with a title at the top. The body of the article can contain text or images or a mixture of both.

- The sidebar on the right side of the page contains 'widgets' (see Lesson 8) which typically contain navigational links to guide the user to other parts of your website. Widgets can also contain text or images.

- The footer is at the bottom of the page. The footer is optional and can also contain widgets.

It often helps to start by deciding what you want your front page to look like. Is this going to be a static 'splash' page introducing your organiza tion or company? Or do you want a blog-type site where the first thing your visitors will see is your latest news or opinion?

What page links do you want to go across the top horizontal menu bar? Again, this will usually remain the same as users click from page to page.

Now think about the header. Do you want a header image? Do you want to upload your own graphic or logo?

What do you want to see in the sidebar? Note that the sidebar is generally used to provide navigation to other parts of your website (or maybe other websites).

Do you want to use footers and, if so, what do you want in them?

As you can probably appreciate, the more work you can do at this stage to plan the layout of your website, the easier and quicker it will be to actually build it.

At this stage your WordPress website is empty except for the sample content ('Hello world!') that WordPress inserts automatically. We'll be deleting that stuff in the next lesson. For now, we'll focus on some of the things you can do to begin making Twenty Twelve look and feel the way you want.

So, log in to your website's dashboard (see Lesson 3) and follow along with me:

Add A Site Title

From the dashboard, go to 'Appearance', 'Themes' and, for Twenty Twelve, you'll see 'Customize', 'Header' and 'Background' as options. (Ignore Widgets and Menus because these will come into future lessons).

Click on 'Customize' and you'll see some drop-down menus on the left side. Now click on 'Site Title & Tagline'. Here you'll enter the title and tagline of your website that will be displayed at the top of every page.

Enter whatever is appropriate for your website (you can change it later if necessary) and click on the blue 'Save and Publish' button at the top left as in Figure 4.3.

Figure 4.3

You can see that this text will now appear in the header of every page of your site.

Select A Color Scheme

Now click on 'Colors'. As you can see, you can change the Header Text color - the color of the text you just typed in. If you have a color-scheme in mind for your website you can begin to make it take shape here. Play around with the color palette box to select the color you want.

In the same dialogue box you can also change the background color. This is set by default to a bluish-gray color but you can change it to whatever fits in with your ideas. I'm going to change my background to black (#000000), because I think it will help my content to stand out on the user's screen. But you can choose whatever color suits your plan – or white if you want to keep it plain and simple. When done, click on the blue 'Save and Publish' button at the top left.

Add A Background Image

As you can see, there is also a 'Background Image' dialogue where you can upload an image instead of having a plain background color. The background image will display in the empty area around and outside the page borders. Whatever graphic you use will repeat itself across, around and behind your web pages.

If you are going to create a particularly jazzy site where the design graphics are an integral part of the image you wish to portray then you might want to explore this option.

I tend not to use background images because I think they can make the screen look too cluttered and can distract the user from reading my sparkling pages(!) – but the facility is there if you want to use it.

Add A Header Image

If you want your site to have a header image you can upload it here. The Twenty Twelve theme does not provide any inbuilt header images and, by default, will not display one. But if you have a graphic that you want to display across your website as a header you can either resize it to 960 pixels width by 250 pixels height on your computer, or upload a graphic of any other size and crop it within this screen. (Ignore the references to the 'Media Library' for now because we will be coming on to that in Lesson 9).

To upload an image, click on the 'Browse' button and navigate to the image on your computer. Then click on 'Open' and 'Upload'. If the image is not 960 x 250 you will be given the opportunity to crop it here. Then scroll down and click on 'Save Changes'. You might want to note here that you can upload a series of header graphics and tell WordPress to display a different header on each page. This could be a great idea if you want a particularly visual-looking website…

I uploaded a header graphic to my demo site and Figure 4.4 shows what the site now looks like:

Figure 4.4

Can you see how the site is beginning to take shape? A few simple tweaks will enable you to begin making your site how you want it to look.

I suggest that you experiment with all the options in this lesson to see how you can change the theme to make it look suitable for the sort of website you want to build. Anything you change here will be effective immediately but you can change things as often as you like, so nothing is cast in stone.

When you've finished customizing your settings, click on the 'Close' button in the top left and this will uncover the dashboard menu items down the left side of the screen.

I'm going to illustrate the rest of the tutorial by using this theme and it will make it easier for you to follow if I keep it as simple as this. And for the sake of further simplicity I have removed the header image above because it will make the illustrations in this tutorial easier to follow.

I will leave my demo website http://1.keepingchickens.net up on the Internet so that you can go in and browse it to see what it looks like after completing this tutorial. (Please note that I know little to nothing about actually keeping chickens so I ask you to cut me a bit of slack on the content…)

FAQ

I can't decide what I want my website to look like! How can I get started?

One way of getting some creative ideas is simply to look at other websites. Find a website that you like the look of and have a good browse around. Note the color scheme and the fonts. Check out the header. See how the site navigation works. How does the site use pictures? Does the site have ads?

Note what you like (and don't like) and see whether you can organize your ideas into a simple structure for your own site. Warning – do not copy other websites or you could be in trouble. And don't get too complicated to begin with. As your site evolves you can add more bells and whistles but when you are starting out the KISS ('Keep It Simple Stupid') principle certainly applies!

Lesson 5. First Steps To A Perfect Website

There's one final job to do before you can start to create a website that is all your own and that's to do a bit of housekeeping and configuration. You need to do this basic setting up so that you clear out the sample content and configure WordPress to work the way you want it.

At this stage don't worry if the details look unfamiliar and puzzling, just follow along and do it and it will all make sense eventually, I promise.

This won't take long and then we can get on with the interesting stuff.

Delete The Junk (Sample Content)

For every new installation, WordPress provides some sample content which you don't really need and which we're going to delete.

When you look at your site you'll see that WordPress has provided the following items on the site:

- Recent comments: Mr WordPress on Hello world!

- Recent posts: Hello world!

- Sample Page

We're going to delete all that and start again. So, from the dashboard, Click on 'Comments'. You'll see the comment displayed as in Figure 5.1:

Figure 5.1

Now, hover your mouse over 'Mr WordPress' and a command line will magically appear underneath the comment. Click on 'Trash' and, hey presto, the comment's gone.

Next, from the dashboard, click 'Posts'. You'll see the 'Hello world' box appear. Again, hover your mouse over it and click 'Trash'. That's gone, too.

Finally, from the dashboard, click 'Pages'. You'll see 'Sample Page' displayed. Hover and trash that, too.

Finally, we'll get rid of a few plugins that we don't need.

Figure 5.2

From the dashboard, click on 'Plugins' and you'll see an item for Jetpack. Click 'Deactivate' and that will make it disappear.

And do the same with 'Hello Dolly'. Delete this plugin and delete all the files. (Hello Dolly is a left-over from the WordPress blogging days and is of no use to us).

We'll deal more with Plugins in Lesson 15 but, for now, that's all you need to do.

Configure WordPress To Behave How You Want

Finally, here's where we check out a few settings to be sure that WordPress is going to behave as we want. Again, don't worry if you don't understand all of this – just do it…

From the dashboard, click on 'Settings', 'Permalinks'. Under 'Common Settings' click the radio button 'Post name' if it is not already clicked. Then hit 'Save Changes'.

Now you have to decide whether you want to allow your visitors to leave comments on your website. This has become a mixed blessing these days because the comments box has become a magnet for spammers and this can be a considerable nuisance. So, I advise you think carefully about whether you really do want to allow visitors to leave comments.

If you do allow visitors to add comments to your pages, by default, a comment box will automatically be displayed at the foot of each page. You have the option of moderating these comments but, if approved, the comments then become an integral part of your website.

To block comments, from the dashboard, go to 'Settings', 'Discussion' and uncheck 'Allow people to post comments on new articles'. Then scroll down and click on 'Save Changes'. That's all you have to do on this page because now all the other settings will be ignored.

However, if you do want comments to appear on your site, check out Lesson 16 where I recommend how to deal with them.

———

Now you've got a completely empty WordPress website ready and waiting for you to populate with your own stuff. And the good news is that, once you have completed Lessons 1 – 5, you don't need to any of this work ever again.

So, with the preliminaries out of the way, let's get moving!

FAQ

Say I want to display a comment box on some pages but not others – is this possible?

Yes – I answer this question in Lesson 16.

Lesson 6. Add Your First WordPress Page

Now, before we begin this lesson, let me just give a brief outline how you should use 'Pages' as opposed to 'Posts', which we will get into in Lesson 7.

Pages are intended to be the 'static' elements of your website, containing content that you always want to be available to your visitors and which, typically, are accessible via a tab on the horizontal menu bar. Think of this as the 'backbone' information. You would typically have an 'About Us' page, possibly a 'Welcome' page, preferably a 'Contact Us' page and, along with that, a 'Privacy' page. Pages do not change very much and you may only need one or two pages.

Most serious websites will have an 'About' page and I recommend that you, too, put up an 'About' page, because it will enhance the credibility of your site.

Add An 'About' Page

Log in to your WordPress website and from the dashboard, click on 'Pages', 'Add New'. Figure 6.1 shows what you'll see:

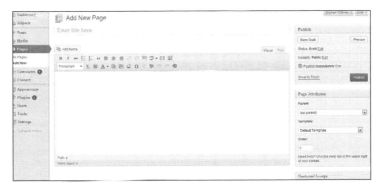

Figure 6.1

Enter 'About Us' (or something equivalent) in the top blank box where you can see the cursor flashing. Then, in the blank box headed by the 'Visual' tab, type some text that describes you or your website or your business. Don't copy and paste the text from somewhere else just yet (I'll tell you why later in this lesson) – just manually type in some text so that you can see how this all hangs together. As you type you'll see that the words wrap round, just like a word processor. If you hit 'Enter', you'll get a new paragraph. Just keep typing until you've got enough text to play around with. Don't worry about how perfect it is, you can edit the page later.

After you've entered a bit of text it's a good idea to click on 'Save Draft'. This is handy when you are setting up a complicated page because it enables you to save your work when you get something right and return to the last draft if (when!) you foul it up at a later stage. I encourage you to use this feature, especially while you are learning. A page saved only in draft is not yet visible to anyone except you.

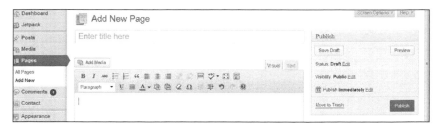

Figure 6.2

Now look at the icons on the toolbar above the text, as shown in Figure 6.2. You'll probably recognize them from other regular text-processing programs that you use.

You can see bold, italic, strikeout, bullets, etc. If two rows of icons don't show, click on the far right icon on the top row and the second row will toggle into view.

The best way to find out what functions these icons represent is to hover your mouse over each of them and then experiment with them. If you hover your mouse over an icon you'll see an explanation of what its purpose is.

The way these (mostly) work is that you select some text, click on an icon and you'll see that change take place. In most cases the operation of these icons is self-explanatory and so I won't include a lot of unnecessary detail here but will let you play around and explore them for yourself. No changes will be made to your website until you click on 'Save Draft' or 'Publish'.

I encourage you to try out the blockquote, spellchecker and links.

To add a link to text in a web page, select a few words in your text where you want the link to appear. You will notice that the little 'chain' icon becomes live and, when you click on that, a small pop-up dialogue will appear prompting you to enter the target URL of the link. See Figure 6.3:

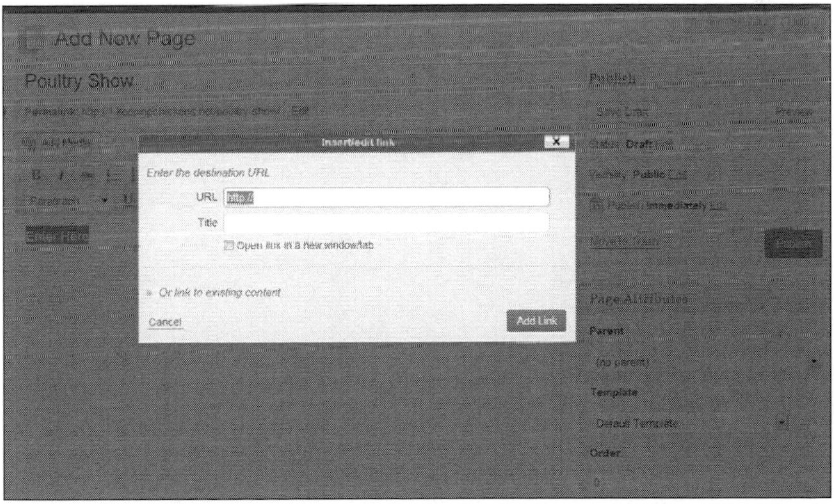

Figure 6.3

The text you selected then becomes a 'hot link' which, when the user clicks on it, will take them to another page, either within your website or to another site.

To see the results of your changes, click on the 'Preview' button over on the top right of the page. You'll then see the web page displayed exactly how it will look on your website.

This 'preview' view will usually open in a new tab in your browser. When you've checked the page over you can close the tab and return to the page where you set it up.

Now, before you publish your page, there is one more feature that you need to check out. The Twenty Twelve theme offers you three different templates for your page layout:

- Default

- Front Page

- Full-width No Sidebar

These are accessible from the 'Page Attributes', 'Template' drop-down box. Try these out one by one and choose the template you want for this page.

When the page is formatted as you want it, you can click 'Publish' and the page will be added to your site for the world to see. You should also notice that WordPress has magically added the page tab to the menu bar above your site header, which is where it should belong.

I now encourage you to think about and add as many pages as relevant to your site. As you add each page you are gradually filling out your site and making it your own!

If your website will consist of a small, finite number of pages then you might be tempted to leave it at that and not make use of posts. But that could severely limit the effectiveness of your website, particularly in relation to search engine optimization (SEO). Posts have a number of very useful features that Pages don't have.

Before we go on to the next lesson, here's the useful tip I promised you to help when copying and pasting text:

How To Copy And Paste Text The Right Way

As you can imagine, it is often easier and quicker to type up your website text offline, in a word-processor such as Microsoft Word or a text-processor like NotePad. But, be aware, just copying and pasting right into the text box on the WordPress page can have unintended consequences.

This is because, when you copy text from your computer to your clipboard, your operating system will often copy not only the text but also the formatting (including fonts) as well. Microsoft Word contains a lot of complicated formatting behind the scenes and this can confuse WordPress because it wants to format the text according to the theme you have chosen and copying unwanted formatting can make it appear all screwy.

So, type up your text offline however you want and copy it to your clipboard as usual. Then, when you get into your WordPress page, click on one of the two little 'T' or 'W' icons in the toolbar ('Paste as Plain Text' or 'Paste From Word') and a pop-up window will appear:

Figure 6.4

Paste your text into this box, click 'Insert' and the text will drop in just like you typed it. This feature applies both to both Pages and Posts.

And there's one more feature that you might like to take advantage of: Parent and Child pages.

Making Use Of Parent Pages And Child Pages

If you have already published at least one page you will see that, under 'Page Attributes', you have the option of selecting a previously published page to be the parent of the one you are currently adding or editing. This means that you can have a hierarchy of pages that you can nest to several levels. If you are planning on building a website with many pages ranging over a wide range of topics this is a feature you might want to use. Parent/child pages appear as such in drop-down navigation menus and can be an easy way of creating a hierarchical structure to steer users around your site.

——

That's about it for Pages; let's find out all about Posts in the next lesson.

FAQ

I want to stop anyone from seeing my website while I'm still setting it up. How do I do that?

As a webmaster, you need to be aware that the prospective audience for your website is both human and robot (search engines). In practice, your website will get few, if any, visitors in the early days and, because of that, I wouldn't fret too much about who can see what.

Ultimately, you will want both humans and robots to flock to your website but, if you really do want to block both of these types until you are ready, you can create an 'Under Construction' page. This page displays to visitors while you get on with setting up the site behind the scenes.

Create An 'Under Construction' Page

The easiest way to do this is to use a plugin called 'Under Construction'. I deal with how to add plugins in Lesson 15, so come back here when you've completed that lesson.

After you've installed the plugin, from the dashboard, click 'Settings', 'Under Construction'. Set 'Activate or Deactivate' to 'on', and leave all the other settings as default. Then click 'Save Changes'. This now places an Under Construction page between you and your visitors. You won't be able to see this page while you are logged into your website yourself so log out and just view the domain URL if you want to see what it looks like.

To prevent the search engines from looking at your setting up efforts, from the dashboard, go to 'Settings', 'Reading' and check the box labeled 'Discourage search engines from indexing this site'. Then click 'Save Changes'. This will tell Google (and the other search engines) that you don't want them to 'crawl' your site to put it in their search results – yet.

And don't forget to undo all of this when you are ready to launch your website!

What if I want to change something on a page after I've published it?

Simple. From the dashboard, go to 'Pages', 'All Pages', and you'll see all the pages you've already published, listed out in date order. Hover your mouse over the page you want to edit and click on the 'Edit' command that pops up. This will take you back to the original page where you can make whatever changes what you want. Then click 'Update'. That's all you have to do. You can edit a page as often as you like.

Lesson 7. Add Your First WordPress Post

You have now added one or more Pages to your website and these provide the static, background information to tell the world about you and your website. Now it's time to start adding content in the form of Posts, which is what will become a more on-going process as you build your website over time.

You will, I hope, be relieved to hear that adding posts is almost the same as adding pages. So I'm not going to repeat all the stuff in Lesson 6. To add a post, just follow the same instructions, substituting the word 'post' for the word 'page' and you'll get there.

The Essential Difference Between Posts And Pages

What I'm going to do in this lesson is point out a few of the differences between posts and pages which might help you make up your mind how the two different types of entries can contribute to your website.

Posts are designed to be a more chronological, dynamic way to present content to your visitors. In the olden days, when WordPress was used primarily for blogging, each post would become the latest in the blogger's stream of news/comments/events. (…'Emily laid one egg today but dear old Jane seems to be getting broody again'…) The latest post would occupy the top position on the page and earlier posts would scroll down beneath it.

Suppose you wanted to have a website where you displayed topical information, or some sort of journal, or news, you'd want to make use of posts. Typically, a website that uses posts also has some static pages (as above) but the Post content includes a series of entries that you add to on a regular basis and which adds further, timely content to the website.

But the real power of Posts is that they also have handy features called 'categories' and 'tags' which I will now explain.

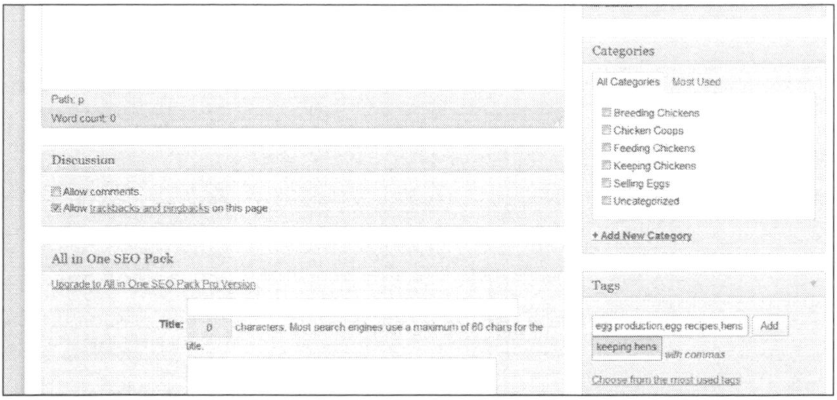

Figure 7.1

How To Make Use Of Categories And Tags

As you will learn, posts don't have to appear on the front page of your website (see Lesson 13). You could have your 'Welcome' page as the front page and, in your sidebar, you could have a series of navigation links filtering your posts by category.

Categories are a way to classify your content into topics so that your visitors can access all the posts you have written on a particular subject. To take my chicken site as an example, I could write a number of posts on broad categories such as 'chicken food', 'chicken houses', 'breeds of chicken' etc.

As I write each post, I would choose one or more appropriate categories for the subject matter. This would then automatically enable me to provide a filter of all the posts in the same category so that my visitors can easily find their way through the site without having to read posts on topics that don't interest them.

If you know what categories you are going to use you can set them up in advance. From the dashboard, go to 'Posts', 'Categories' and add them there. But you can also add categories as you go by adding a new category at the time you add a post, as shown in Figure 7.1.

Tags are a looser way of categorizing your material that will help the search engines associate certain keywords with your posts. Every time you add a post you should add two or three tags which contain keywords or phrases to help the search engines classify your site. And one way to use the tags you have coded is to have a 'tag cloud' in your sidebar. I'll show you how to do that in the next lesson.

Before I leave the subject of posts, let me share another neat feature of WordPress: the ability to pre- and post-date entries.

How To Go Back (Or Forward) In Time

If you simply want your post to be dated at the date and time you published it then just leave it. But if you want to backdate an entry, you can change the date of publication to a prior date.

Just above the 'Publish' button, where it says 'Publish immediately', click on 'Edit' and you can change the date and time to whatever you want. Change the date/time as shown in Figure 7.2 and click on 'OK'. That's the date/time that will appear on your website.

Figure 7.2

And, hey, you can even schedule WordPress to publish a post at some date/time in the future. Just change the date (as in Figure 7.2) to a date in the future, click 'OK' and 'Schedule'. WordPress will hold the post until that date/time occurs and then it will automatically publish it as if you had hit the button yourself. Magic!

Using Quickpress

As we have seen, there is a shortcut you can use to add new posts. From the dashboard, look at the box marked 'QuickPress', as shown in Figure 7.3.

You can quickly add a new post with title, text, tags and even a picture and publish this immediately.

Figure 7.3

So, now you can begin adding Posts to your website, complete with categories and tags, continuing to add them until you have the range of content you need to display a full and rich website.

———

Next, we're going into the final lesson of the Quick Start Guide where I'll show you how to use Widgets to enhance your WordPress website.

FAQ

I've added some posts and now I realize that they should really be pages. Can I convert a post into a page (and the other way round)?

Sadly no. The way out of this is to copy the text from the unwanted post/page, add a new post/page and paste the text that you just copied. Then delete the unwanted page/post.

How do I delete a post or page?

See Lesson 5 (Delete The Junk).

Lesson 8. All About Widgets

Now that you have your website loaded up with some content, it's time to add a few refinements to make your site appear useful and well-designed. You can do this by inserting widgets in the sidebar of your website.

What are 'widgets'? Widgets are very handy little chunks of functionality that perform common tasks. You, the webmaster, choose which widgets you want to use to perform additional tasks to improve your website's appearance and performance.

Examples of widgets include:

- List of categories in your website

- Links to your latest posts

- Custom menus

All these widgets are clickable hotlinks that guide your visitors around your site.

As you can see in Figure 8.1, I have put into the sidebar of keepingchickens.net the Categories, Recent Posts, Archives and Tag Cloud widgets. It's up to you what you use on your site because, as you can see, there are a lot of widgets to choose from.

Figure 8.1

One of the primary functions of widgets is to provide different ways of navigating your site. But you can also add text widgets that not only display text but which can contain computer code. We'll cover these text widgets in Lesson 11.

The number and position of the widgets you can use will depend on the theme you are using. The Twenty Twelve theme allows you to insert widgets into your sidebar and, optionally, up to two footer areas across the bottom of a static front page.

Other themes may allow you to put widgets in your header area or at the bottom of individual pages.

Here's how to set up widgets:

From the dashboard, click on 'Appearance', 'Widgets'. The 'Widgets' screen is shown in Figure 8.2:

Figure 8.2

Add Some Sidebar Widgets

In the previous lesson we discussed using categories when writing posts. You can group all your posts into categories by placing a 'Categories' widget in your sidebar. When a visitor clicks on a category they will be shown only your latest posts in this category – they won't see posts in other categories that do not interest them.

The really neat thing about this widget is that it all works completely automatically. You don't have to do anything except to code your posts with the required category: WordPress takes care of all the sorting and filtering for you and the widget will update automatically.

I encourage you to experiment for yourself and see what the widgets fit in with your ideas for your own site.

To insert a widget into the sidebar simply click and drag it from the main body of the screen to the 'Main Sidebar' box over on the right. When you do this, a 'Save' button will pop up and all you have to do is click that and you're done. You will see that there are often options with widgets and you can usually insert your own titles. When you have saved a widget, click 'Close'.

If you want to rearrange the order of the widgets in the sidebar simply drag and drop them, up and down, until you have them as you want. You don't even need to save the sidebar: it stays as you last left it!

Please note that widgets won't work unless you have already set up the content that you want to display. For example, a 'Recent Posts' widget won't display anything until you have actually added some posts to your website.

The easiest way for you to find out what widgets can do for your website it to experiment. Play around by clicking and dragging widgets into the Sidebar and Footer Areas and see how it looks. You can add and delete widgets as much as you wish.

Delete Unwanted Widgets

If you want to delete a widget from your sidebar, simply click on it and then click 'Delete' and it will disappear. You can always add the widget back in again if you change your mind.

FAQ

Can I have different sidebar widgets on every page?

By default, WordPress will display the same widgets on the sidebar of every post or page. There is a good reason for this: it provides a consistent visual 'map' of your site to your visitors so that they can more easily find their way around regardless of where they browse.

But some themes do enable you to design more than one sidebar and then choose how and when to display them, so this is not cast in stone.

If your theme doesn't provide this and you have a good reason for wanting to display different widgets in the sidebar on different pages of your website, there is a useful plugin called Custom Sidebars that you can use to achieve this. Plugins are covered in Lesson 15.

What if I don't want a sidebar on my website?

Then just delete all the widgets. If you don't have any widgets, no sidebar will be displayed.

———

That's it for the Quick Start Guide. Have you made a start on your website yet? NO? Lessons 1 - 8 are all you need to get your website up and running, albeit in a very simple format. So I urge you to go back to Lesson 1, make a start and just do it. It gets easier once you make a start, I promise.

Building a website may seem an uphill challenge but, actually, it's quite good fun and you'll get a great sense of achievement when you see your very own domain come to life…

If you have made a start on your website, then congratulations – welcome to the community of WordPress webmasters! The In Depth Guide will take your web building skills to the next level. See you in Lesson 9!

IN-DEPTH GUIDE - DRILL DOWN TO THE WONDERS OF WORDPRESS

Lesson 9. Add Images To Your WordPress Website

WordPress has some very powerful and flexible ways of handling media on a website and, in this lesson, we are going to look at several ways of doing so

First, some background information. WordPress provides a folder within your website called the 'Media Library' (Figure 9.1) which can contain images, documents, downloadable files etc. This is the depository of all of the images (and other media) that you have uploaded for use in your website.

Figure 9.1

Media files are labeled either 'Attached' or 'Unattached', depending on whether or not you have actually used the media by linking to it from one of your posts or pages.

Adding a picture into a post or page to illustrate your text is one way of making your webpage look attractive and relevant. If you upload the picture when adding a post or page WordPress automatically loads it into the Media Library and it becomes an 'attached' image.

If you want to add an image for use later, you can upload it directly into the Media Library as an 'unattached' image and then call it whenever you want it.

To add an image to a page or post, you need to have the image file stored on your computer as a JPEG, GIF or PNG file type, sized in pixels that will fit on your page and generally less than 8 megabytes in size.

WordPress is quite flexible in handling images and will happily resize your picture to fit the available space in a post or page. But it's worth just checking out the default settings for image sizes because your website will look more professional if you present your images in consistent shapes and sizes.

To do this, from the dashboard, go to 'Settings', 'Media' (Figure 9.2) and check out the pixel dimensions that WordPress will use when displaying your pictures. The standard 'medium' size is maximum 300 pixels height and width. If your theme is wider than about 1000 pixels you may want to increase this to 400 or 500 pixels to display your images larger.

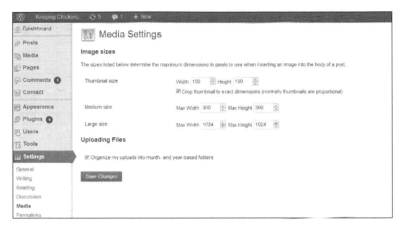

Figure 9.2

If you change the Media Settings be aware that the settings will apply only to images you insert after this: WordPress won't retrospectively apply the settings to any images you have already inserted on posts or pages.

Add A Picture To A Post Or Page

To add an image to a post or page, first click on the point in your text where you want the image to appear. This can be anywhere within the text: right at the beginning, or in the middle of a text block or after the end. The image will be embedded exactly at the point you select here.

Then click on the button labeled 'Add Media'. A pop-up box appears, prompting you to locate the file you want to upload. You'll see that there are two tabs, 'Upload Files' and 'Media Library'. Click on 'Upload Files' if this is not already displayed.

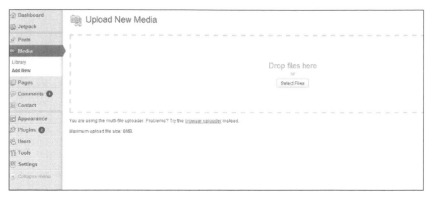

Figure 9.3

As you can see from Figure 9.3, you can actually drag and drop the file(s) you want to insert but I'll demonstrate the alternative, which is to upload from your computer.

Click on 'Select Files' and navigate to where you have stored the image on your computer. Click on the file you want to upload, and then click 'Open'. A screen as in Figure 9.4 appears:

Figure 9.4

Here you can see that the screen displays all the images I have already uploaded to my Media Library, with the latest one checked on the left and the 'Attachment Details' for the latest image on the right.

Now you can enter the title of the image, optionally a caption, alt text (alternative text to display on devices that don't display images) and description. Entering descriptive details in these boxes will help the search engines index and classify your images and relate them to the text that you enter in your posts and pages.

Beneath this is the 'Attachment Display Settings'. Here you can specify the alignment of the image – left, right, center or none. I encourage you to experiment with alignments because you can get some very striking effects with the right image in the right place.

You will also see that there is a 'Link To' box. This is where the visitor would be taken if they clicked on the image. You can change this link to anything you like: if this was a product you were selling you might replace this with a link to your order page.

If you leave the 'Link URL' unchanged and the visitor clicks on the image they will see a full-pixel version of the image on their screen. If you don't want the image to be a link then click on 'None'.

Finally, you can choose the size of the image within the post or page. Your options here are determined by the settings you specified earlier in this lesson. Again, experiment with this to get the effects that you want for your website.

Then click on 'Insert into Post' and Figure 9.5 shows what the page will look like:

Figure 9.5

Now let's have a look at uploading images directly into the Media Library for use later.

Add A Media File To The Media Library

Sometimes you will want to add an image (or some other media) to be displayed somewhere on your website other than a post or a page. In that case, you need to upload it to the Media Library before you can use it.

For example, I have a graphic file on my computer that is actually a little banner that I want to place in my sidebar to advertise a product that I want to promote on my website. I will cover how get the image into the sidebar in Lesson 11 but here I'll briefly show you how to upload the image to the Media Library:

From the dashboard, click on 'Media' / 'Add New'.

Click on 'Select Files' and upload the image as before.

As before, it is good practice to enter a title, alternate text and description, which will help with SEO (see Lesson 18) then click on 'Save all changes'. That's it. The file is now stored on your WordPress Media Library, ready for when you need it.

Add A Featured Image

This is a relatively new WordPress facility which lets you associate an image with a post or page. At the time of writing, featured images are not used in every theme and different themes use them in different ways. However, Twenty Twelve does use featured images and this is how to use them:

Essentially, the featured image facility in Twenty Twelve enables you to insert an image above the post/page title and below the header image (if present) and site title. If you do not have a header image for your site and you upload a similar-sized image (960px x 250px) as a featured image to a post or page, it will effectively become the header for that post/page only.

In the screen where you add or update a post or page, you will see at the bottom of the right-hand menu a box labeled 'Featured Image'. Click 'Set featured image' and you will be taken to a screen similar to the ones illustrated above, where you can either upload an image or use one from your Media Library. Click on 'Set featured image' and you will see the image thumbnail appear on your post/page. That's all – save/update your post/page but do not insert the same image into your post/page or it will display twice!

When you view the page you will see your image at the top.

Add A Picture Gallery

If you are a photographer or an artist or anyone who wants to display a lot of pictures, you might want to add a gallery of pictures to a page or post. A 'gallery' is a way of displaying thumbnails of images on a page in a rectangular grid and when a visitor clicks on an image they can see it full size.

In this case, it is preferable to prepare the images first on your own computer, so that they are all the same orientation and size (in pixel dimensions). That way the gallery display will look professional.

Before adding a gallery you should decide what size you want to display thumbnail images. By default, the thumbnails will be 150 pixels x 150 pixels. But you can change this by going from the dashboard to 'Settings', 'Media'. This will display the Media Settings screen and you can change the dimensions of how WordPress will display thumbnail images on your site.

Then, from the page or post where you want to display the gallery, click on the 'Add Media' button as before, but this time select multiple files to upload. You will see WordPress upload them one at a time to the Media Library.

Make sure that all the pictures you want are checked and then click 'Create Gallery' over on the top left of the screen. Then click 'Create a new gallery' in the bottom right of the box, then 'Insert Gallery'. The big blue gallery icon will be displayed. You can add text before or after this icon.

Then Save or Publish your post or page and you can then view the page to see the gallery, as in Figure 9.6:

Figure 9.6

As you can imagine from what you've seen, there are actually a great many options for displaying images and other media in WordPress, some of which are rather specialized and would be of interest to people like photographers and graphic artists etc.

Also, there are a number of very fancy plugins you can use to display images in a slideshow or gallery that go way beyond the basic facilities shown here. And some themes offer a 'slider' function that can include some very dramatic effects.

In this lesson I have shown the basic methods of adding images and media that you are most likely to use in a regular website. As ever, I encourage you to explore the options further for yourself if you want to be a bit more adventurous.

FAQ

I added an image to my post but how can I move it to a different position?

In the 'Edit Post' page, click on the image that you want to move and drag it to where you want it. If that doesn't work, click on the image and then click on the small 'Edit Image' icon that appears in the far top left of the picture. This displays a pop-up which allows you to edit the alignment, link, title, caption etc. Make what changes you want and then click the 'Update' button.

Or, if you want to start over, click on the image, hit the delete key on your keyboard, insert the cursor where you want the image to appear in your text and insert the image over again.

Then click 'Update' to update the post or page.

How can I get one of those moving slideshows on my website?

There are a number of very good plugins that will display a slideshow of images and it is worth experimenting with several to find the one that suits you. Some slideshow plugins will display the gallery (see above) associated with a post or page while others will require you to upload your images separately.

One slideshow plugin that I currently like is called 'Portfolio Slideshow' because it is relatively easy to set up and there is also a low-cost 'pro' version of it available. See Lesson 15 for how to find and install plugins.

Lesson 10. Add A Video To Your Website

Videos are now a popular feature of many websites and WordPress makes it quite easy to include them in posts or pages.

For reasons which I explain in the FAQ below, I do not recommend that you upload videos to your Media Library. Instead, I suggest that you upload the video to YouTube (or one of the other white-listed video-sharing websites) and link to it from your website.

WordPress now provides a very easy way to display a video on your website from third-party video sites. Here's how.

First of all, find the YouTube (or wherever) video that you want to use (yours or someone else's) and click on it:

Figure 10.1

In your browser's menu bar you will see the URL of your chosen video. It will look something like this:

http://www.youtube.com/watch?v=UgZg_6oq3EU

Copy this URL to your clipboard.

Then go to the post or page where you want to display the video and, on a line of its own, paste the URL of the video just where you want the video to appear.

Don't make this into a hyperlink: just leave it as a line in the text.

WordPress knows that this is an approved video site and will translate the URL into an embedded video. Magic, or what?

When you view the page it will look something like Figure 10.2:

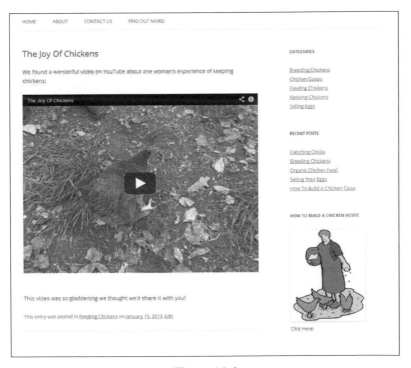

Figure 10.2

The frame of the video is shown in the content of the post/page and when the visitor clicks on the 'Play' button the sound and picture plays from YouTube.

FAQ

How can I add a video that I recorded myself?

It is possible to embed your own video files into a WordPress website but you do need to be aware that videos can be very large files and there is a file size limit of 8 megabytes that you can upload via WordPress into your Media Library. This restriction severely limits your options for displaying self-hosted videos.

And, because video files are usually very large and eat up bandwidth, if you have a basic hosting plan you may find that your hosting provider will want to charge you extra if you want to host your own videos on your own website.

The easiest way to show videos on your site is to upload the file to YouTube or Flickr (or any of the many other free video hosting sites) and use the code that they provide (as example shown above) to embed the file into your post or page as shown above. But if you really do need commercial video hosting there is always Amazon Web Services (aws.amazon.com) who, for a fee, will provide a powerful video serving facility that is used by many of top-name webmasters.

If you don't want to do it this way and your file size is less than 8mb then I suggest you search for plugins that will do the job (see Lesson 15). I won't recommend any particular plugin because there are new ones coming out all the time and they all differ in what they can do and how. But spend some time experimenting with plugins until you find what you want.

Be aware that you may need to use HTML to do this job and so you should also study Lesson 19 where I show you how to do this.

In the next lesson we'll be looking at how to enhance your website with text widgets. This cool feature gives you endless options of adding more functionality and making your site unique.

Lesson 11. The Power Of Text Widgets

We looked at the basics of Widgets in Lesson 8 but there are a number of other things you can do with widgets that will provide much more functionality.

The best way to see what widgets in general can do is to experiment with the options available (from the dashboard, click 'Appearance', 'Widgets'…) and view the results. As before, all you usually have to do is drag the widget into the appropriate area on the sidebar, configure the options and save it. If you don't like it, you can delete it.

But there is one widget that will provide almost endless variations and possibilities and that is the Text Widget.

Basically, the text widget enables you to insert text into your sidebar or other areas of your website, but the good news is that the text can also be computer code: HTML and JavaScript in particular, instead of simply plain text. When WordPress sees that the text is actually computer code, it executes it and renders the results where you have placed the text widget.

This facility can, for example, enable you to display graphics and ads in your sidebar and here I'll show you how.

Add An Image Using A Text Widget

There isn't, as yet, a simple WordPress widget that lets you place a picture in the sidebar but it can be done easily enough with a bit of HTML. This example will include an easy piece of HTML code that you can copy and edit into a text widget that will place a graphic in your own site.

The first thing you need to do is upload the image file to your Media Library (see Lesson 9) and copy the File URL of the image file to your clipboard.

The easiest way to construct the HTML for this to type it into a text editor such as NotePad. So type this piece of text (exactly!) into NotePad:

<img src=" " />

and then place your cursor between the two quotation marks and paste the File URL you just copied to the clipboard into that space. This is what this looks like for my chicken keeping site:

<img src="http://www.keepingchickens.net/wpcontent/uploads/2012/01/keepingchickens.jpg" />

Now, go to 'Appearance', 'Widgets' and drag a text widget to the sidebar where you want to display that file. Then copy and paste the snippet of NotePad text into the text widget, 'Save' and 'Close'.

View your site to see the results. Figure 11.1 shows what my site now looks like, with a little graphic image in the sidebar:

Figure 11.1

Use A Text Widget To Display A Banner Ad

One of things that webmasters like to do is to use space on their website to advertise products, either their own or someone else's. They want to place a small graphic (a 'banner') in the sidebar of their website which is clickable, and which will send the visitor through to a sales or order page.

If you are advertising a third-party product, the merchant or agent will often provide the complete code to display the ad. All you have to do is to copy and paste it into a Text widget, as in the previous example. Then click 'Save' and 'Close' and the banner will display where you placed it.

But what if the product or service you are advertising is your own, or the advertiser wants you to host their graphic on your website?

Advertisers sometimes do this because it saves them bandwidth. What you need to do in this case is to download the banner graphic from their website and upload it to your site's Media Library (see Lesson 9).

The method of displaying the banner graphic is the same as the previous example but the difference is that you want the image to be 'clickable', that is, the code must include a link.

I will illustrate this by actually making the image on my website a clickable link. I'll make the target of the link a sales page of a product that my visitor could buy.

The advertisers have given me the URL of the link I need to use to direct the visitor to their sales page.

The outline HTML code to display a clickable image looks like this:

```
<a href=" " ><img src=" " /></a>
```

In between the first set of quotation marks you need to paste the URL of the webpage where you want to send your visitors when they click on the image. Between the second set of quotation marks paste the File URL of the image in your Media Library.

So, the HTML for this on my chicken keeping site is:

<a href="http://tuetwo.chickcoop.hop.clickbank.net" >
<img src="http://www.keepingchickens.net/wpcontent/uploads/2012/
01/keepingchickens.jpg" /></a>

This is illustrated in Figure 11.2:

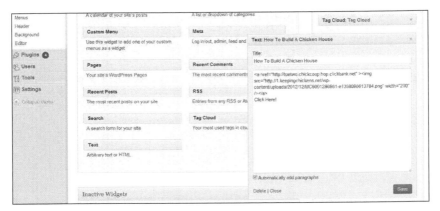

Figure 11.2

I leave you to play around and experiment with text widgets on your website. All you have to do (in most cases) is to drag and drop the widget into your sidebar, 'Save' and 'Close'.

FAQ

How do I show Google Adsense ads in my sidebar?

AdSense ads are the little the chunks of code links you see on many websites which advertise goods and services available from third parties. This is a program run by Google where people pay them to display ads and Google pays web publishers (you!) to display them.

You have to sign up with Google as an AdSense publisher and then you are allowed to display AdSense ads on your site and (hopefully) get paid for doing so.

You have to have a completed website which is getting some traffic before Google will allow you to sign up to AdSense. But once accepted you can display ads on any site registered to you.

Google provides snippets of Javascript code for you to display text and image ads in various shapes and sizes, depending on where on your site you want to display the ads. A 'skyscraper' or other narrow vertical format would be suitable for a sidebar.

Drag and drop a text widget into your sidebar (or anywhere else you want to display ads), copy the Javascript code and paste it into the text widget. Then click 'Save' and 'Close'. Google then displays ads related to the content of the page it is displayed on.

———

Now let's get on to another vital element of a successful WordPress website: Custom Menus.

Lesson 12. Custom Menus And Why You Should Use Them

Custom Menus are a relatively new feature of WordPress but they add a lot of flexibility and power to the design of a WordPress website.

What Is A Custom Menu?

If you look at most websites you will see that they have somewhere a row of tabs which consist of links to pages or areas within the site. This row of tabs is called a 'menu'.

Figure 12.1

As shown in Figure 12.1, menus are often in a prominent position at the top of the page and their labels provide clues as to where you will be taken if you click on them.

Before Custom Menus were introduced, WordPress would automatically create a menu from all of the pages in your website and, every time you added a page, another tab would be added to the menu. The menu would be displayed wherever the theme placed it, usually somewhere across the top of the page.

The problem was that, if you had a lot of pages (or pages with long titles), your menu would become very crowded and could even confuse your visitors.

By default, this is how WordPress will still behave. If you have only a few pages in your website then maybe this is sufficient and you may not need to have Custom Menus.

But if you want to choose what goes in your menu and/or decide whether to have more than one menu, then you should make use of custom menus.

How To Create A Primary Menu

A 'Primary Menu' is one that your theme has already configured into its design. The Twenty Twelve theme has built this into the horizontal menu bar at the top of the page, as shown in Figure 12.2. Other themes may designate the primary menu as links or buttons down the right or left sidebar, or elsewhere on the site.

Figure 12.2

To construct your primary menu, from the dashboard, click on 'Appearance', 'Menus'. In the box labeled 'Menu Name' type a name for the menu (it doesn't matter what the name is) and click 'Create Menu'. I've created a menu called 'blank' in Figure 12.3:

Figure 12.3

You can see that there are a number of options here that make this a very powerful feature:

- 'Custom Links' are links to anywhere you like: a page, post or even a picture inside your site, or a link to another website. Type the full URL of the location you want to link to, enter the 'Label', which is the text that will appear on the menu tab and click 'Add to Menu'. You can add as many of these as you like to the menu.

- 'Pages' enables you to pick and choose from the pages you have so far published. The beauty of this option is that you can put some pages in one menu and some in another. Check the pages that you want to include on this menu and click 'Add to Menu'.

- 'Categories' refers to the categories recorded on Posts. If your website consists mostly of posts you can have a menu that enables your user to browse selected categories from your menu.

As you can see, you have to check the items that you want to include on the menu and click 'Add to Menu'. You can mix and match the different types of menu items in one menu if you like.

If you want, you can also change the 'Navigation Label' to a different title than the one that would appear as default. Expand the menu item by clicking on the down arrow to see the box where you can do this.

The items within the menu can be dragged and dropped into the order you want them to appear, and another neat option is that, if you have a lot of items in the menu, you can arrange them into a hierarchy by simply dragging pages slightly to the right and they will nest beneath the ones above.

When the menu items are assembled how you want, just click 'Save Menu' and it's done.

Now you must tell WordPress that you want this menu to appear as your site's 'Primary Navigation' which, in the case of the Twenty Twelve theme, is horizontally across the top of the page. Under 'Theme Locations', select the menu that you just created from the drop-down list and click on 'Save'.

How To Create A Secondary Custom Menu

In addition to the Primary Menu, you can create additional menus that you can display in the sidebar or other areas of your site. When you have a lot of pages, or categories, or other destinations where you want to send your visitors, this can be a useful way of dividing the navigation of your site into more meaningful sections.

For example, you could have the more important and interesting pages in the Primary Menu up at the top but other, less important, pages such as Privacy Policy, Terms of Service, Site Map as a secondary menu in less visible locations such as the sidebar or front-page footer (see Lesson 13).

To create another Custom Menu, from the dashboard, click 'Appearance', 'Menu' and click the tab marked with a + at the top of the screen. (See Figure 12.3)

Then enter another menu name, as before, and click 'Create Menu'. You can then populate that menu with the pages, Custom Links or categories that you want and click 'Save Menu'.

Position Your Custom Menus Using Widgets

When you have created a secondary custom menu you can position it where you want it by using the 'Custom Menu' widget.

To do this, from the dashboard, click 'Appearance', 'Widgets' and drag a Custom Menu widget into the sidebar or other widget area provided by your theme, as shown in Figure 12.4:

Figure 12.4

Select the menu to appear in that space and then click 'Save'.

As you can imagine, the possible combinations and variations on how you can use this are endless.

———

I hope I have demonstrated some of the ways you can use Custom Menus, but you can experiment for yourself and discover how you can use this feature to make your website look and behave the way you want.

FAQ

Help - I have just changed the theme on my website and my custom menu has disappeared! What's happened?

First, you need to check that your new theme actually supports custom menus. Most up-to-date themes do, but there may be a few who have yet to catch up with this recent feature.

If your theme does support custom menus then read on.

When you change your WordPress theme the new theme may not automatically register that you have set up a custom menu so you have re-set the primary menu. From the dashboard, click 'Appearance', 'Menus', 'Theme Locations'. Select your primary menu from the drop-down list and click on 'Save'. That tells the theme that you do have a custom menu and it should then display it, as required.

Lesson 13. Set The Home Page Of Your WordPress Website

One of the differences between building a WordPress website and creating one using traditional HTML-type tools is that WordPress lets you choose which page you want as your front (home) page. This is the first page that visitors will see when they land on your domain.

Traditional webmasters sometimes have difficulty getting their head around this: if you are one of them, just forget everything you ever knew about index.html...

By default, WordPress will choose to display your latest posts. This is fine if you have a 'journal' or 'latest news' or 'blog' type of website. If you leave it as the default or if you choose 'your latest post', your front page will be updated every time you add another post. This was how it worked when WordPress was (and still is) used for a traditional blog.

But if you want a static page as your front page you have to say which page you want.

Set An Existing Page As Your Home Page

To set your front page, from the dashboard, click 'Settings', 'Reading'.

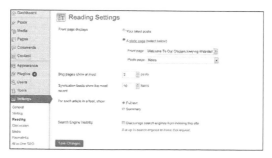

Figure 13.1

To set an existing (static) page as your front page, click the appropriate radio button as shown in Figure 13.1, select the required page from the drop-down box and click 'Save Changes'. This page will then become your home page.

2012 Front Page Template

The 2012 WordPress theme provides an optional special template for you to use for your front page. This does not have a sidebar but instead has two separate widget areas beneath the main article on the page.

What this means is that you could, for example, construct a 'welcome'-type page and then show a sub-set of navigation links in the two widget areas. You can then lead your visitor into the areas of the site that you would like them to visit first.

I have done this on the front page of my chicken keeping site as shown in Figure 13.2:

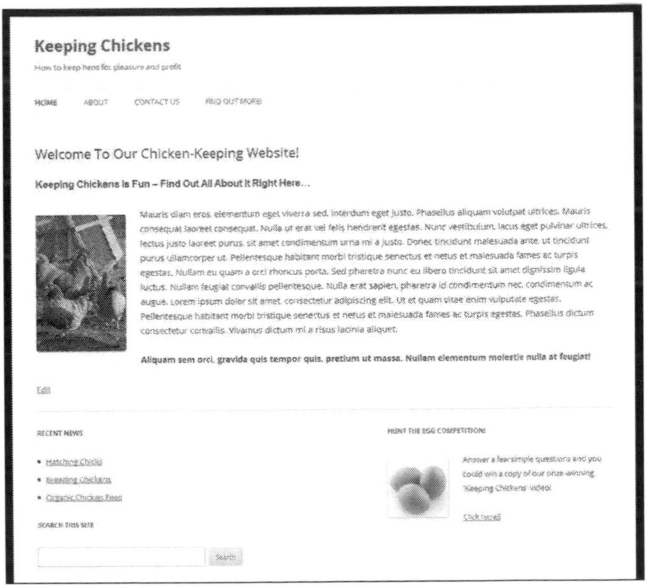

Figure 13.2

Group Your Posts On To Their Own Page

There's also another optional, handy feature that I like to make use of. If you set a static page as your front page then you can have all your posts grouped together on another 'container' page which can then appear as a tab on the menu bar. This means that you don't then need to have a widget in the sidebar to show the latest posts.

To do this, just create a blank page with the heading you want as its title and publish it, either as a blank page or maybe a small amount of text as an introduction.

You could, for example, create a blank page with the title 'News' or 'Blog' or something equivalent. Then, on 'Settings', 'Reading', select that page from the 'Posts page' drop-down box. This is illustrated in Figure 13.1.

Then, whenever you add a post, it will automatically be added to that page.

Set The Number Of Posts To Scroll

Whenever you add another post to your website, by default, the latest post will occupy the space at the top of the page and all older posts will scroll down beneath it. Because of this it is a good idea to decide just how many posts you want to see scrolling down the page. If you want your website to look more like a conventional site maybe one will be enough. WordPress initially sets this number to ten which is probably too many for most purposes.

So, to set the number of posts per page view, from the dashboard, click on 'Settings, 'Reading' and set the indicator labeled 'Blog pages show at most' to the number of posts you want to see on the page.

Again, this is illustrated in Figure 13.1 where you can see that I have set my 'News' page to display three posts.

This setting will be applied whether or not you have a static front page.

When you're done, click on 'Save Changes'.

Set A Sticky Post

Another useful feature of posts is that you can designate one of your posts to be 'sticky', which means that it will always appear above other posts of a later date. This can be very handy if there is some permanent information that you always want to display ('How To Order'…) on the top of your front page but to have later posts scrolling beneath it.

To make a post sticky, on the Post page, click on 'Edit' next to 'Visibility' and check 'stick this post to the front page'. Then click 'OK', as shown in Figure 13.3.

Figure 13.3

When you publish or update the post, it will always appear on the front page of your posts.

FAQ

I want a fancy front page with a rectangular grid showing excerpts and links to my site's featured posts. How can I get that?

You are talking about what is known as a 'magazine' theme. This lets you select a particular page template to use on your site's home page which presents excerpts and thumbnails to selected posts. Magazine themes usually come with many options to configure and customize how you want the content to appear and they often use some advanced WordPress options.

There are some good free magazine themes available on WordPress: check out Bombax, Pureline and BirdSITE, although there are many more.

If you want to go down this route, I recommend that you experiment with free themes to start with because there can be a learning curve in working out the best way for you to display your particular content. When you know what you want you can investigate some of the available premium magazine themes which can provide some truly impressive results.

Lesson 14. Choose And Change Your WordPress Theme

WordPress themes are the design templates that determine the appearance of the website. There are hundreds (thousands?) of free themes to choose from and you can (usually) switch the theme quite easily if you change your mind about what you want.

You should be aware that the Twenty Twelve theme that we have used to illustrate this tutorial only offers a sub-set of the possible options that WordPress provides to present your online content.

For example, some themes offer more than one header widget, others provide sliders and galleries, and some have built-in functions like opt-in boxes while others can format your content in a magazine-like view.

So, if you think that your requirements are too complex for WordPress to render, I urge you to think again and explore some of the more feature-rich themes that some very clever designers have provided for you.

Figure 14.1

WordPress offers many free themes on its website that you can install with a few clicks of the mouse. Others are offered by third parties, some for free and some for sale.

You can commission a professional to create a unique theme just for you or you can even create your own themes by the use of drag-and-drop software such as Artisteer.

See the Conclusion of this tutorial to find out where to read more about these options.

But to illustrate the possibilities, we are going to go to the WordPress site and pick a free theme.

Install A Free WordPress Theme

From the dashboard, click on 'Appearance', 'Themes' and then the 'Install Themes' tab.

You'll see a menu where you can search for available themes:

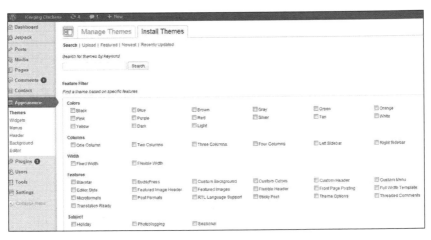

Figure 14.2

If you know what shape and color of theme you want, then click on the appropriate check boxes and then click on 'Find Themes' to see what comes up.

Alternatively, you can browse the latest offers. You could click on the 'Featured' tab because these themes are usually very striking and will often suggest ideas for how you might build your site.

Three free themes that I currently use are 'Responsive' (see Figure 14.1), 'Graphene' and 'Pageline'. These all get very good reviews from their users and they have clean and original designs that I happen to like. If you know the name of the theme you want you can search for it in the box at the top of the above screen.

When you find a theme that you like the look of you can click on 'Preview' to see how the theme will look on the screen. This will pop up in a new window which you can close when you've seen enough. It's also a good idea to click on the 'Details' links to see how many stars the theme has been awarded by other users — the more the better.

When you've found a theme that you like, click on 'Install' and then on 'Install Now' in the pop up window. This will automatically upload the theme to your website. You can now preview the theme again as it will look on your own website and, if you like it, click 'Activate' and you're done — you've changed the theme.

You can change the theme of your WordPress website as often as you like, but it is a good idea to do your experimenting early on in the development of your site. What you ideally want is to find a theme that fits the style and personality that you want to portray and then settle down when you are comfortable with it. Your visitors will soon come to recognize the look and feel of the website with your particular style.

If you change the theme more than once you will probably end up with several non-active theme files in the background. You can, if you wish, go back and re-activate a theme that you've previously installed. But, when you know that you don't want to make use of a previously installed theme, it's a good idea to simply delete it because it will just be taking up space on your web hosting server.

After installing a new theme, have a look at the options it gives you for changing the header, widgets, colors, or whatever. The theme's author may provide a link to their website where you can find out more about this theme or others that they may have on offer.

Install A Third-Party Theme From A Zip File

If you have a theme that you have obtained from a third party, you will likely have the theme files in a ZIP file sitting somewhere on your computer, in which case do not unzip it.

To install a zipped theme from your computer, from the dashboard, click on 'Appearance', 'Themes', 'Install Themes' and then click on the 'Upload' tab, as in Figure 14.3:

Figure 14.3

A pop-up box will prompt you to browse your computer to locate the ZIP file and when you have done so, click on 'Install Now'. The theme should then upload and install automatically from the ZIP file. Activate it, as above, and you're done.

———

OK, I've made it look pretty simple to choose and change your website's theme, but there are one or two important provisos that you need to be aware of.

If you choose a theme and then go on to do a lot of work on your website (particularly with widgets and menus) and then decide to change your theme, the new theme may not automatically pick up all your content and display it how you want.

It may be just fine, but be aware that this is a possibility and you may have to reinstall your widgets and/or menus. This is not usually a big deal but it may just cause a bit of unexpected work.

WordPress issues new software releases from time to time and sometimes these are major upgrades which require a theme to be upgraded accordingly. Most reputable theme designers keep their themes up to date but be aware that you may be forced to change your theme if your designer's theme gets out of sync with the latest WordPress release.

FAQ

How can I design my own theme?

To design your own theme you need to be fairly competent at CSS, HTML and PHP, not to mention graphics technology and WordPress. So, to be realistic, it isn't easy for a beginner to design their own WordPress themes.

However, one easy way for a non-geek to create a unique WordPress theme is via software that lets users design WordPress themes using a very flexible template which they can then tweak and personalize themselves. I use Artisteer to do this and I thoroughly recommend it. It takes a bit of practice to explore all its possibilities but I use it a lot to create my own, unique themes. See the Conclusion to find out more details of Artisteer.

What's a 'child theme'?

Child themes are rather beyond the scope of this tutorial, but I will briefly explain what they are and how they can become useful.

Essentially, a child theme enables you to create a theme that inherits most of its characteristics from another theme (the 'parent' theme) but which contains a few specific changes that make it different from its parent. For example, if you have a parent theme that has a sidebar on the right but you want a sidebar on the left, you can create a child theme that specifies sidebars on the left.

You do this by creating a small style sheet file (style.css) that contains the changes that you want to override the corresponding lines in the equivalent parent theme's style sheet.

The principle is that the original parent theme remains unchanged and can be subject to updates and enhancements but the child theme's style sheet will always be linked into the parent and the changes will still apply at run-time.

This is a relatively new attribute of WordPress and their development team has stated that child themes will become more important as future WordPress updates occur. At the very least, it will probably mean that tools will become available for non-tech users to tweak and personalize their themes without having to risk compromising the functionality of the underlying theme.

So, watch out for more announcements from WordPress about child themes.

Lesson 15. The Power Of Plugins

'Plugins' is a term for a collection of additional (often free) pieces of software that provide extra functionality for WordPress websites. These are the 'optional extras' that you may, or may not, need to make your website behave as you want.

They are called 'plugins' because they do exactly that: if you install a stand-alone plugin, WordPress detects that it's there and makes the connection with it automatically. You may have to configure a few parameters to tailor it to your requirements, but that's all you have to do.

There are thousands of WordPress plugins available but, in this lesson, we're just going to install a few of the ones that I consider essential. They are all free. I will explain what they do and how to use them as we go along.

First, I'll show you how to install plugins in general. Then, I'll list my recommended plugins and show you how to configure them.

How To Install Plugins

From the dashboard, click 'Plugins'. You should see the list of currently installed plugins as in Figure 15.1:

Figure 15.1

To install any plugin, from the dashboard, click 'Plugins' then 'Add New' at the top of the screen. You can access the plugins you need several ways from here, but the quickest way is to click on the 'Popular' tab and see what comes up, as in Figure 15.2.

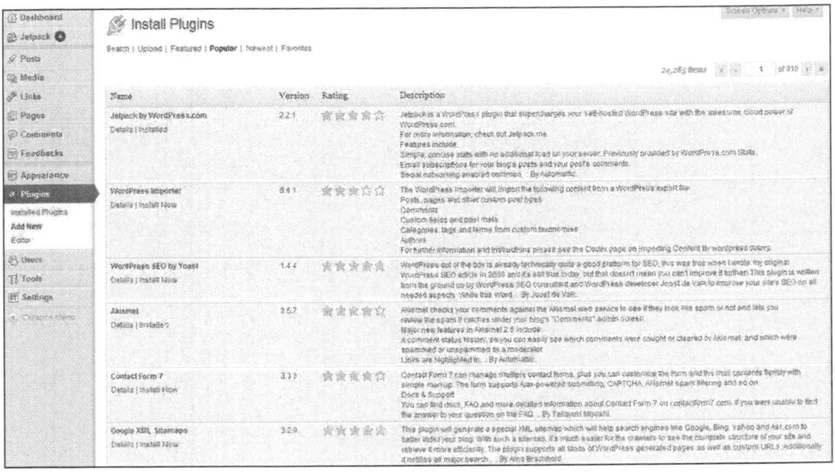

Figure 15.2

You will probably see some of the recommended plugins straight away.

To install a plugin, all you have to do is click on 'Install Now' on that plugin's listing and confirm that you really do want to install the plugin. Then WordPress takes over, installs the plugin on your website automatically and then all you have to do is activate it.

You should repeat this step for all the recommended plugins that you can find on the first page of 'Popular'.

If you can't find the plugin on the 'Popular' page, then the other way of locating a plugin is to search for it. Instead of clicking on 'Popular', use the 'Search' box on the 'Install Plugins' page. Type the exact title of the plugin into the Search box and click 'Search Plugins'. You may be presented with more than one choice so be sure to pick the one that has the exact title, and then install the plugin as above.

Recommended Plugins

So, the plugins I recommend are:

Google XML Sitemaps

This popular plugin provides a Google-compliant sitemap for your website.

What's a sitemap? Well, it is a file called sitemap.xml that sits in the background on your website and which contains a complete list of all your website's pages and posts and documents the connections between them.

The sitemap file is there for the benefit of the search engines, to help them find their way around your site and index it accordingly. Sitemaps are not really for human visitors!

Most professional websites have a sitemap and this plugin is considered to be essential for effective SEO.

The plugin updates the sitemap automatically every time you add, delete or edit something so, once installed, you don't have to do a thing.

All In One SEO Pack

This, in my opinion, is another essential SEO plugin. It provides all the features you need to optimize your site's pages to rank in the search engines for your chosen keywords.

When you install the 'All In One SEO Pack' plugin and activate it you will see a red warning prompt at the top of the screen asking you to configure the plugin. See below for instructions on how to do this.

Contact Form 7

Having somewhere on your site where your visitors can contact you is considered good practice and makes you look serious and trustworthy in your customers', and the search engines', eyes.

Simply sticking up an email address on your website is not a good idea because it will quickly be harvested by the spam phishers and your email address will rapidly become unusable.

This plugin provides a secure way for people to contact you privately and will provide the credibility you need to present a professional face to the world. Later in this lesson I will show you how to create a 'Contact' page.

———

OK, we're nearly done. Just let's finish by configuring the plugins we just installed. If the plugin doesn't appear below, then the good news is that there's nothing more to do on it!

Configure All In One SEO Pack

Click on the link on the red prompt message at the top of your website page and you'll get to the options page for this plugin, as shown in Figure 15.3:

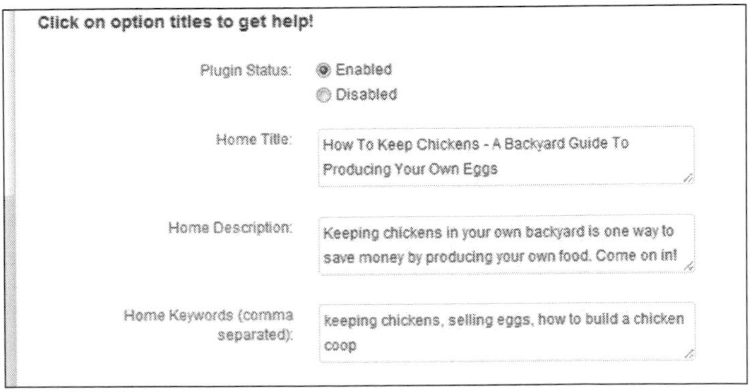

Figure 15.3

First, click the radio button next to Plugin Status, 'Enabled'. Then look at the three boxes below entitled 'Home Title', 'Home Description' and 'Home Keywords'. These are the boxes that tell the search engines what your site is all about.

The text you enter here will show up on the search results when your site appears on their listings. Figure 15.3 shows what I entered for my website.

Enter your text and scroll to the bottom of the page and click 'Update Options'. There are a lot of other technical options available on this page and it is safe to leave the defaults as they are.

Now that you have installed this plugin you will notice that it has added some similar boxes to the individual Pages and Posts screens:

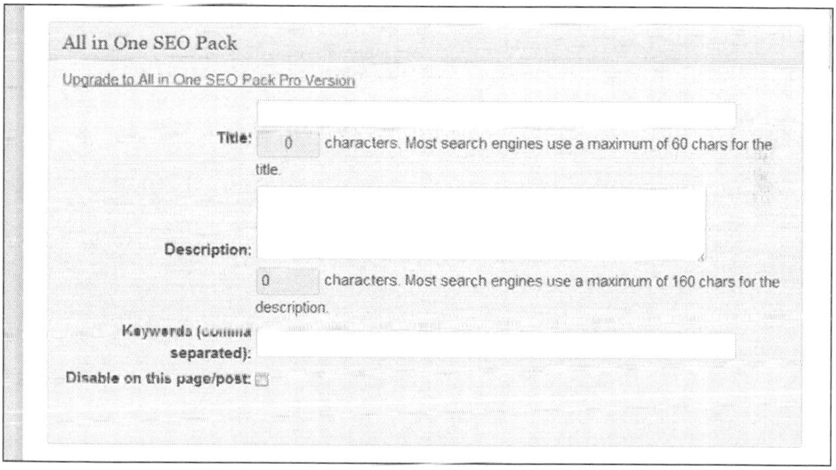

Figure 15.4

The fields 'Title', 'Description' and 'Keywords' shown in Figure 15.4 are what is known in tech-speak as 'meta-data'. This information gets copied to the invisible background of your webpage and is provided solely for the search engines; your human visitors will not see this information.

It is good practice to fill these each time you add your pages and posts. I will cover this topic again in Lesson 18.

Configure Contact Form 7

From the dashboard, click 'Plugins' and click 'Settings' for 'Contact Form 7'.

There is nothing really to change here, but it would be a good idea for you to check that the email address quoted on this page is the email you want your messages to be sent to. This will not appear on the contact page and will not be visible to anyone other than you. If necessary, change this email address and then click on 'Save'.

Before leaving the page, copy the shortcode at the top of the page ([contact-form-7 id="55" title="Contact form 1"]) to your clipboard.

Add A Contact Page

Now, let's quickly add a 'Contact Us' page. From the dashboard, click 'Pages', 'Add New'. Enter a title such as 'Contact Us' and then paste the shortcode you just copied into the body of the page. You can add some surrounding text if you like, and then click 'Publish'. Easy – you just got yourself a 'Contact' page.

While you are going through this exercise you may well see other plugins that look interesting and that you are tempted to install. By all means explore what's available and install more plugins if you can see a use for them. My advice, when looking for plugins, is to choose only those with three or more stars and do not install a plugin that has not been tested with the version of WordPress that you are using.

You can find out more about a plugin by clicking on 'Details' against that plugin on the 'Install Plugins' page.

———

There are many, many more plugins that you can use and I leave you to discover and install them yourself. But a quick word of advice if this is the first WordPress website you have ever built. Don't overload your website with plugins if you cannot justify that they are necessary for the functionality of your site.

Plugins can clutter up your site and slow it down and can, from time to time, conflict with one another. And, as with themes, plugins can become out of date and can stop working if the plugin's author has not kept up to date with the current version of WordPress. So, take it step by step and be a little self-disciplined in your use of plugins, at least at first.

FAQ

What is the best plugin for keeping track of the number of visitors to my website?

'Google Analytics' is the system used by most professional webmasters and this provides an extensive breakdown of how many visitors your site attracts and where they come from.

To use Analytics you need to have a Google account (free, and easy to set up) and you have to sign up to Analytics. All this is explained in http://www.google.com/analytics/.

When you have added your website to your Google account, you are provided with a snippet of tracking code which you have to include on your website. This operates in the background and invisibly monitors your visitors so that Google can present you with a detailed breakdown of your website traffic. You can see the daily results of this by logging into your Google Analytics account.

There are various plugins which enable you to add the tracking code to your website and the one I currently favor is 'Google Analytics for WordPress'. Search for this plugin as explained above, install it and copy and paste your tracking code as directed.

Having said all this, when you first get started Google Analytics may not be very useful because you may not actually be getting many visitors. So, you don't need to rush into this until you have your site up and running (say, after a month or so).

Lesson 16. Comments: Start A Dialogue With Your Visitors

You may remember that, in Lesson 5, I cautioned you about allowing people to comment on your posts and pages because of the nuisance of spam. Leaving open the opportunity for visitors to add their own content can turn your website into a magnet for spammers around the world to post garbage and, at times, some seriously offensive material.

Enable Comments

However, if you have a good reason for inviting your visitors to leave comments on your website, and if you are prepared to moderate it, here is what I recommend you do:

From the dashboard, click on 'Settings', 'Discussion' and check the following boxes:

- Allow people to post comments on new articles

- Comment author must fill out name and email

- An administrator must always approve the comment

- Comment author must have a previously approved comment

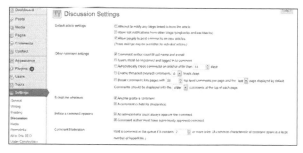

Figure 16.1

As you can see from Figure 16.1, there are other settings on that page that are self-explanatory and you can decide for yourself what else you want to check.

Then click 'Save Changes'.

That's all you need to do if you want a comment box to appear at the foot of every post and page. But you will probably want to be a bit more selective about which pages you actually want to allow comments on. For example, you probably wouldn't want to invite comments on your Contact page.

To set up selective commenting, from the dashboard, go to 'Pages', 'Add New'. Then look over to the top right of the screen and click on the arrow next to 'Screen Options' as in Figure 16.2.

Where it says 'Show on screen' make sure the 'Discussion' box is checked.

Figure 16.2

What this will do is to add a 'Discussion' box on the screen where you add a new page. You can then check or uncheck whether you actually want a comment box on that page at the time that you add or update that page.

Do the same with the Screen Options on the 'Posts', 'Add New'.

Moderate Comments To Banish Spammers

Note that I recommend that comments must be approved before appearing on your website.

The way this works is that, when someone posts a comment via a page or post on your site, the administrator (you!) will receive an email informing you that a new comment is awaiting moderation.

You then have to approve the comment before it is published. When you approve a comment it will appear on the page where it was originally posted. But if the comment is spam you can mark it as spam and it will disappear.

If a visitor posts a comment and you approve it, then, if that visitor ever visits your site again and uses the same email address, they can post another comment which will be automatically approved. That's because WordPress assumes that you trust this visitor and that their future comments are going to be OK.

This is generally true but a few people do abuse this so it's a good idea to just keep an eye on comments. You can easily trash any that are unwelcome.

Moderating comments yourself will probably be all you need to do in the early days of your website because the volume of user comments will likely be manageable. But what if the spammers find you and you are suddenly overwhelmed by hundreds of spam comments?

The answer is to use a plugin to filter the comments before they even get through to your site. The anti-spam plugins I use and can recommend are:

- Akismet

- Spam Free WordPress

- GASP

You will only need to use one of these plugins to filter spam. Akismet is the most popular (and, in my opinion, the most reliable) but you will have to pay a small license fee if your website is for commercial purposes, otherwise it is free.

At the time of writing, each of these plugins is available and up-to-date but I recommend you check them all out and select the one that seems most appropriate for you. To find out more about each of them, search for them by name as described in Lesson 15.

FAQ

If someone posts a comment on my website, can I post my own reply to that comment?

Yes. You can, in effect, enter into a dialogue with your commenting visitors. When anyone adds a comment to your site and you approve it, a 'reply' link will appear alongside it. To enter your own reply to that comment, display the post/page where the comment appears, click on the 'reply' link and another comment box will appear for you to add your reply.

Help - I have set my site to allow comments but no-one has ever added a comment! What am I doing wrong?

Relax – in the early days of a website you will probably not be getting many visitors and those who do visit may just be passing by. And even when you do get traffic, in most cases only a very small percentage of visitors will actively contribute their own comments.

Give it time. Post regularly to your site and try to build up a regular readership.

Why not add some controversial topic and ask your readers to have their say? You could even invite your friends to chip in and start off a discussion. Just keep at it!

Lesson 17. Users And Their Capabilities

By default, WordPress assigns the role of 'administrator' to the user (you!) who created the WordPress installation. The administrator is the person who has the capability to do everything with the website – add, amend, delete pages, posts and media, change the theme, set passwords, install plugins, manage widgets and add or delete other users – and more.

As a user, you have a profile. To see yours, from the dashboard, click 'Users', 'All Users' and you will see your username listed. Hover the mouse over your username and click 'Edit' when it pops up. You'll see all the information that WordPress knows about you, as shown in Figure 17.1:

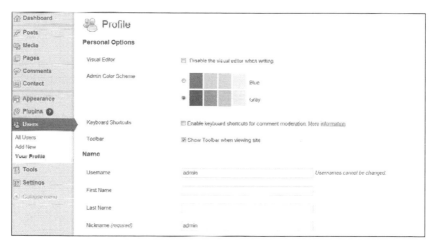

Figure 17.1

You don't have to add any more information if you don't want to but, if you do, some of the information may be visible to visitors to your site.

Note that here, at the bottom of the page (Figure 17.2), is where you can change your password. This is the password you need to login to the WordPress dashboard and you can change this whenever you want to.

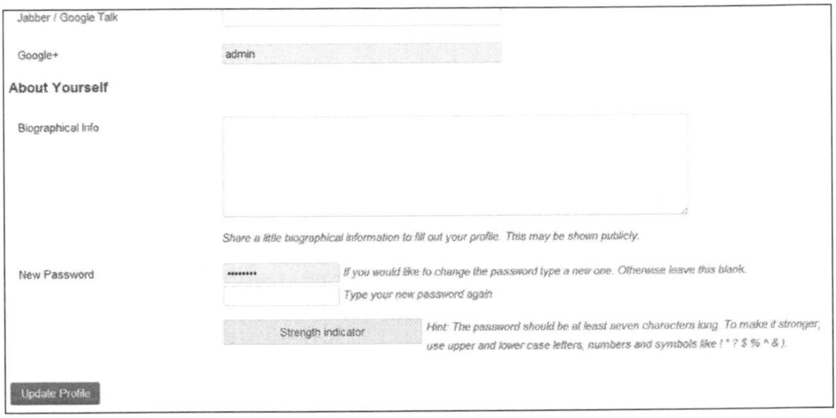

Figure 17.2

Just type in the new password (twice) and then click on 'Update Profile'.

If you are the founder of your website and you will be the only person who ever works on it, then you can now safely skip the rest of this lesson.

But if there could be more than one person working on the site then you will need to know how to create other users.

Add Another User

To add another user, from the dashboard, click 'Users', 'Add New'. As you can see from the screen, the fields at the top of the screen (User-name, E-mail, First Name, Last Name etc) are self-explanatory. Enter all you need to identify that user. At the bottom of the screen is a drop-down box marked 'Role'. This will tell WordPress what that user is, and is not, allowed to do on the site:

- Administrator - somebody who has access to all the administration features (the same as you!)

- Editor - somebody who can publish and manage posts and pages as well as manage other users' posts, etc.

- Author - somebody who can publish and manage their own posts

- Contributor - somebody who can write and manage their posts but not publish them

It is up to you to decide how to allocate the role and capabilities of each user to suit your organization and team.

When all is filled in, click 'Add New User' and you're done. That person can now login to the WordPress dashboard (see Lesson 3) with the username and password that you have assigned and will be given the capabilities that the role permits.

FAQ

I set my friend up as a user on my website so that he could be a contributor, but he's forgotten his password. How can I retrieve the password for him?

The easiest way for you to do this is to set a new password for him and here's how to do it.

Log into your website as the administrator. From the dashboard, click on 'Users', 'All Users', hover over your friend's name and click on 'Edit'. Scroll down the page and enter a new password (twice). Then click 'Update User'.

Then email your friend with the new password and tell him not, under any circumstances, to forget it again…

Lesson 18. Search Engine Optimization (SEO)

As I have mentioned, SEO is a huge topic and is all about how to optimize your website to attract visitors. There is no point in having a state-of-the-art website with all the bells and whistles that make it work like a dream if no-one ever visits it.

So you need traffic, which is a technical term for real people, with real eyeballs, eager to view the delectable content you have prepared for them.

Now when we talk about SEO we really mean optimizing websites for the Google search engine. Google isn't the only search engine but it is the biggest, and what Google does, the others follow.

The basic problem that all webmasters face is that there are literally billions of websites on the Internet all competing for attention. When someone goes on to Google and performs a search, they begin by keying in some sort of query, for example, 'how do I keep chickens in my backyard'.

Google checks its index and instantly displays ten results on the first page, as in Figure 18.1:

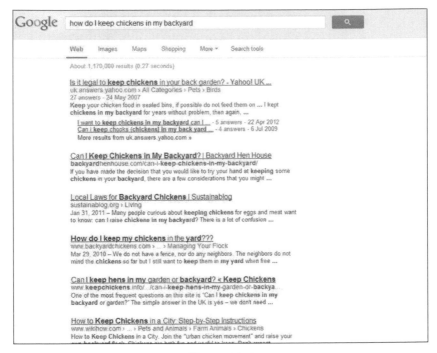

Figure 18.1

If the user sees what they want they'll click on a site. If they don't, they might just move over to the second page, but rarely beyond that. So, if your website doesn't show up on the first couple of pages of the search, you are invisible.

Now, wouldn't it be great if your website could appear on page one or two of the Google search results when someone types in a query applicable to your site? That's really what SEO is all about.

Google has traditionally been quite guarded about how they decide which websites deserve to appear prominently on their search results. Their search algorithms have always been one of the big trade secrets of this billion dollar enterprise.

But now canny webmasters have effectively reverse-engineered the algorithms and found ways of effectively 'gaming' the system to trick

Google's computer robots (that we techies have dubbed 'spiders') into artificially boosting their sites.

To deal with this, Google regularly issues new versions of its algorithms and they have lately been a bit more informative about what we webmasters can actually do to please their mighty spiders.

So, while I cannot give you all the insider intelligence on how to definitively optimize your website (nobody outside of Google can), what follows here is a summary of the latest tips Google has now magnanimously released…

Firstly, what I can tell you is that Google likes WordPress websites because the WordPress behind-the-scenes code forces the site to be neat and tidy, without broken internal links, and with a spider-friendly structure that makes it easy for them to crawl the site. So, choosing WordPress is one big plus for you!

Basic WordPress SEO

These few simple steps will optimize your WordPress website so that Google and the other search engines will have every incentive to index your site efficiently and thus help you attract targeted traffic. All these tips start from the dashboard:

'Settings', 'General'

'Site Title' is very important. As shown in Figure 18.2, it should contain (preferably start with) the main keyword that you want to optimize for. For example, 'Keeping Chickens' is much more precise and descriptive than 'Joe's Backyard'.

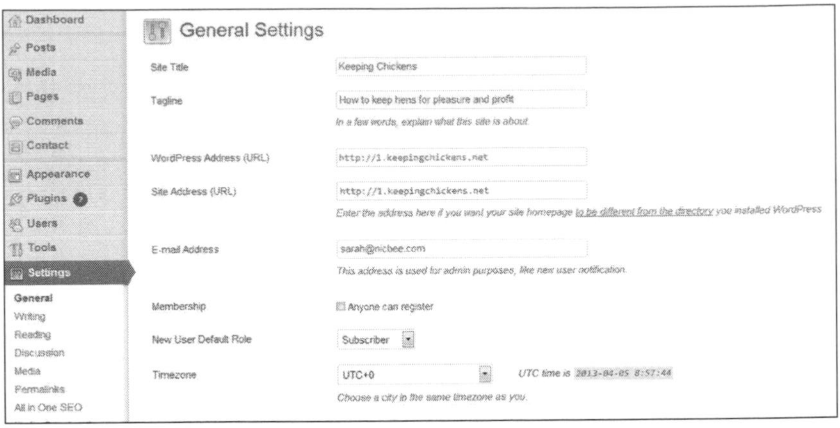

Figure 18.2

Once your site begins to attract traffic don't change this unless there is a good reason to do so.

'Posts'/'Pages', 'Add New'

The post or page title is also important. Again, this should contain one of your site's main keywords. Make sure that the permalink accurately records that. Edit it if it doesn't.

The content of your post/page should be unique and should contain a sprinkle of words or phrases which have a connection or association with the keyword(s) in the post/page title. The main keyword(s) should be included in the text a few times but not to an exaggerated extent.

One of the latest features that Google looks for is whether your page is useful and interesting. One of the ways it measures this is by looking at how long your visitor stays on the page, how many pages of your website they read and whether they share the content with others. If people tweet or like or share your web pages on social networking sites like Twitter and Facebook then that boosts Google's approval.

Google also likes to see the main body of your text above the fold. This means that the user need not have to scroll down the page to find anything readable. If the top half of your page is taken up with ads then that's a downer.

Google also likes the text to be grammatically correct with no typos or spelling errors.

If you have a long article on your post-page you should consider using sub-headings, again containing one of your keywords. Use the drop-down 'Paragraph' box to format subheadings as 'h3' (not h1 or h2 which your theme might use for other purposes).

If you have an image embedded in your text, add your keyword(s) to the image title, description, alternate text and, optionally, caption.

In the case of Posts, use one or more relevant categories and add two or three keywords to Post Tags.

Remember that you have to do two things when writing your posts and pages. You must communicate effectively not only with your human visitors but also to the computer robots (spiders) that try to work out what it is that you are talking about.

All in One SEO Pack plugin

This plugin is important for SEO because it specifically adds what is known as 'metadata' to the internal coding of your site. This is not visible on the page to human visitors but it's there, behind the scenes, for the spiders to gobble up.

In the plugin's boxes on the Pages and Posts pages (See Figure 15.4 in Lesson 15), enter the post/page title, a summary of the post/page content in the description and three or four keywords. The 'description' box is the text which will be displayed by the search engines on the search results page (see Figure 18.1) so you need to write this in plain language, with keyword(s) appearing naturally in the text and, preferably, a call to action. ('Find out how to build a chicken coop here!')

If you want to know more about this plugin and the ways in which it can help with your SEO have a look at the documentation provided on the plugin's website.

——

That's the basics from me on this topic, but I encourage you to explore more for yourself because SEO is important for all webmasters to understand.

FAQ

What's a 'keyword'?

A keyword is one or more words that might trigger a match in the Google Search Engine database.

Here's how this works. When you first build your website, Google (and all the other search engines) find your website and their software robots read ('crawl') the words on each page, especially the headings and anything you've made a point of emphasizing. The bots ignore all the HTML and technical stuff – all they're interested in is the actual words that you have written in your pages and posts.

They deliver this data back to Google's indexing software which then analyses what you've written and decides what your website is all about. This is very powerful software and it generally does a pretty good job of impersonating a human reader.

Google then stores the information about your website in its vast database, waiting for someone to sit down at their computer and type a query into their search page which might match what your website is all about.

So, if you want your website to be found by your target audience then it's important that you optimize your content for the keywords that they might use when searching for information. And that's where we come to the other side of the equation.

The term 'keyword' also denotes the words that the user types in as their query.

Google saves every string of words that users type in to find something and their software calculates the frequency with which these phrases or combinations of words occur, over all the searches made. Therefore, they can calculate very accurately how popular a particular topic or phrase is. And, as you can deduce, the more popular the keyword, the more difficult it is to get your website to come up on page one because there will be too many competing websites.

For example, golf is a very popular topic that people want to search for. But simply typing in the word 'golf' is usually a waste of time because it is too broad. Millions of people simply type in the word 'golf' and Google does its best to come up with something relevant but the user could be looking for anything and the results they get will likely be too broad to be useful. And it would be virtually impossible for you to get your website to come up on the first page of Google when someone simply types in 'golf' because there are just so many other well-established websites competing on the same subject.

But here's where the 'optimization' bit comes in. Canny surfers have come to learn that they'll get results quicker if they search for something more specific, for example, 'golf shoes'. But even that is very broad.

It's much better to look for 'men's golf shoes' or even 'men's blue golf shoes' or 'men's blue golf shoes size 10'. That narrows down the search and the user is more likely to find what they're looking for.

So, if you're selling golf shoes, it will be easier for you to rank your website in the search results if you optimize one or more pages for very specific words and phrases to describe exactly what products you have for sale.

'Sportco Men's Blue Leather Golf Shoes Size 10' tells Google, and your potential customer, precisely what you have for sale. And you will have a much better chance of coming up higher in the search results simply because there is much less competition for these keywords.

But what if you are a small business or organization and you just want your website to publicize your name and brand?

SEO is much easier if your name is unique (or nearly) because there is much less competition. If your website is all about 'Clarissa Clancy Clairvoyant' then it's much easier to appear on page one of Google when someone types in your name because you are probably the only one using that keyword.

But that presupposes that you have done enough publicity to get your name known outside of Google in the first place – and that's quite another topic!

Lesson 19. Behind The Scenes With HTML

Right at the start of this tutorial I said that you don't need to know HTML to use WordPress. This is true, but you can see from a couple of the previous lessons that it can be handy to know how to insert HTML if you need to use it to display something not covered by WordPress.

HTML stands for 'Hyper-Text Markup Language' and is the code that, originally, people had to use to create and maintain a regular website.

The beauty of WordPress is that it shields you from all this in its user interface but, behind the scenes, WordPress generates all the necessary code for you. And it does it (mostly) very efficiently.

I'm not going to teach you HTML here but I'm going to show you how to use it if you have written any of your own code or if you have a code snippet provided for you to perform some function not supported by WordPress.

Add HTML Code To A WordPress Page

WordPress presents you with an alternative window to use on Posts and Pages if you want to insert your own code. To do this, click on the 'Text' tab in a post or page, as in Figure 19.1:

Figure 19.1

When you click on that you are taken to the HTML window and WordPress expects that there will be some HTML or other code included in the text.

You can write any text as normal and WordPress will display it as normal, but when it encounters any HTML it will execute it rather than displaying it as text.

Figure 19.2 shows the text box with HTML code in it...

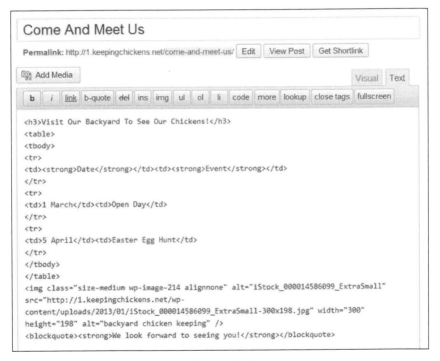

Figure 19.2

... and Figure 19.3 shows what that page looks like to the visitor:

Figure 19.3

When you use this Text tab there can be occasions when WordPress doesn't render the HTML code as you might expect. This is because it does a further layer of verification before accepting the code and this can mean that it strips out anything that it doesn't like.

This can be annoying, but you can force WordPress to accept your code if you temporarily change your User profile.

Disable The Visual Editor

From the dashboard, go to 'Users', 'Your Profile' and you'll see a screen like Figure 19.4:

Figure 19.4

Check the 'Disable the visual editor when writing' box and then scroll down and click 'Update Profile'.

Now you can enter the code you want into your post or page and it should retain the code 'as is' when you publish it.

If you do this, you will have to go back to your User profile and uncheck this box if you want to re-enable the visual editor for use in future posts.

But you'll have to remember to repeat the disabling if ever you want to go back to edit the original post because, if you don't, WordPress will strip out all your code!

———

I suppose I ought not to leave this lesson without a health warning. Inserting HTML code into a WordPress post or page can have unintended consequences. This can be because the HTML code may contain an error, or maybe something in the code clashes with the site's theme, or simply that you are trying to do something that WordPress considers to be invalid.

If you get problems with HTML you have two choices: remove the offending code, or call for help from someone who knows what they are doing.

FAQ

I'm a total non-techie and all this stuff gives me a headache. Do I really need to know about HTML?

No. You don't have to worry your pretty little head about it at all, if you don't want to. You can leave it to WordPress.

Lesson 20. How To Be A Winning WordPress Webmaster

OK, this section of the book is for when you have completed Lessons 1-19 and you have a working website up and running. People in this situation often ask me, 'Right, I've done my website, now what next?'

Well, I'll let you into a little secret. Successful websites are never really finished. The point about a living website is that it reflects change through time and it is always up-to-date and fresh when visitors land on it. So, work on a winning website never really stops.

Build Up Your Website

So, you should embark on a schedule of constantly adding new pages and/or posts and fine-tuning your site navigation so that visitors can easily find the information they are looking for.

The more work you do, the more skilled you will get at it and you will effectively learn on the job. And, trust me, you will find it very rewarding to see your website coming to life.

Get Feedback

When you're ready, ask others to give you an honest appraisal of your efforts. Find out what else they would like to see on the site and whether they can offer any positive suggestions for improvements.

Promote Your Website

Don't forget the external promotion of your website. You need to let everyone know about your website by adding your domain URL to all your publicity material and your email signature and your business cards and your profile on forums etc, etc.

If you are on Facebook or Twitter or Google+ or LinkedIn (or any other social media), make sure that all your friends, followers and contacts know about the website.

Where possible, ask others with websites to link to yours as this will help your search engine visibility.

Expand Your Skills

And, as you work away, you will find that your skill-set will grow. You will discover that you have mastered techniques that you once thought unfathomable and you will also gain the confidence to learn even more. That is, essentially, how I learned WordPress and you can do the same.

Get Help

As it says in the title, I wrote 'WordPress To Go' as a guide for beginners, not a definitive work on the whole topic of WordPress. But I hope that I have equipped and encouraged you to find out for yourself the answers to questions not covered here.

WordPress has its own self-contained, contextual 'Help' system. Look at the top right of each of the pages in the dashboard and you will see a little 'Help' tag. When you click on that you will see a drop-down box that contains text and links to provide more information about the type of page you are on and how to use it.

In addition to WordPress.org, there are many other websites offering useful information about WordPress.

Go on to Google and simply type in the question(s) that you want answered. Make sure you include the word 'WordPress' somewhere in the question.

You may be surprised at how much information there is out there for free. You will understand a lot more from that material after you've been through these lessons than you would have done before.

But one warning about picking up WordPress tips from external websites. Check the date of the page or article that you are referencing because WordPress information can quickly go out of date.

If what you are reading is more than one year old, be careful that the information you are reading is still current.

Finally...

So, my message in this final lesson is to keep at it. Expand and polish your website. Keep it all fresh and up-to-the-minute. Keep on learning. And take pride in your achievement.

That's the way to become a winning, WordPress webmaster!

Conclusion

WordPress is a huge topic and I hope that you have found this tutorial a useful guide to getting you started. I have deliberately kept things as simple as possible and, for that reason, I have not ventured further than the essential first steps.

Thousands of people with no previous web experience have used this tutorial successfully - and I look forward to you joining them!

If you've reached this page but you haven't yet made a start on creating your own website then please, go back to the beginning of this book and work through it again. If it all seems a bit confusing the first time through, then the details will likely all begin to click into place the second time around. Give it another shot and you'll soon be well on your way to getting your very own website.

If you have followed these lessons and created your own website on your own domain then congratulations – you did it! You have made a start in getting your own online presence and you are now, officially, a webmaster.

Further Resources

As I have mentioned, the WordPress scene changes all the time with more new updates and features than I can possibly include in this book. I have tried to cover the very basics in this tutorial but you can find more tools and tips on my website where I add any information that I think will be useful.

You can find a load of recommended resources on my website at http://wordpress2go.com/resources/ where I have listed many more sources that you can investigate. And if you have a genuine query about something in this book then you can contact me via this site and I will do my best to answer.

Also on my website I have listed some of the places you can go to find more WordPress themes, other than the free ones available from WordPress. I have also provided details of some of the tools, free and paid, that I have found useful in building my own websites.

I have also left my demo site http://1.keepingchickens.net online so that you can view it and see the results of this tutorial in real time.

Please Review This Book!

Finally, please let me ask you a favor. If you have found this book useful, please would you go back to 'WordPress To Go' on Amazon and leave me a review? Satisfied readers provide the very best advertisement for a product and I would value your opinion.

We all like to see helpful reviews when we are looking to buy something and it's good for everyone if customers are willing to share their opinions.

——

Again, thank you for using my tutorial. Good luck with your website!

About the Author

Sarah McHarry is a webmaster, programmer and writer.

She built her first WordPress website in 2008 and, as a professional webmaster, accustomed to battling with the intricacies of HTML, PHP and CSS, it was a revelation to her.

Here, at last, was an interface that made web-building accessible to everyone. Better still, it was free and available to anyone who wanted to use it.

Sarah has since built dozens of WordPress sites, both for herself and for her clients. And one of the unexpected outcomes of creating all those WordPress websites and blogs for her clients was that they began to ask how they could set up and maintain their sites themselves.

This is how this book came into being.

After experimenting with a number of methods to present the information, Sarah found that the '20 Lessons' format was the most effective.

This book is the result.

When she is not fiddling around with websites, Sarah likes to play bridge, take photographs and indulge in guerilla gardening.

Sarah is British (but half-Canadian) and currently lives in the West Country of England with her cat, Fanny.